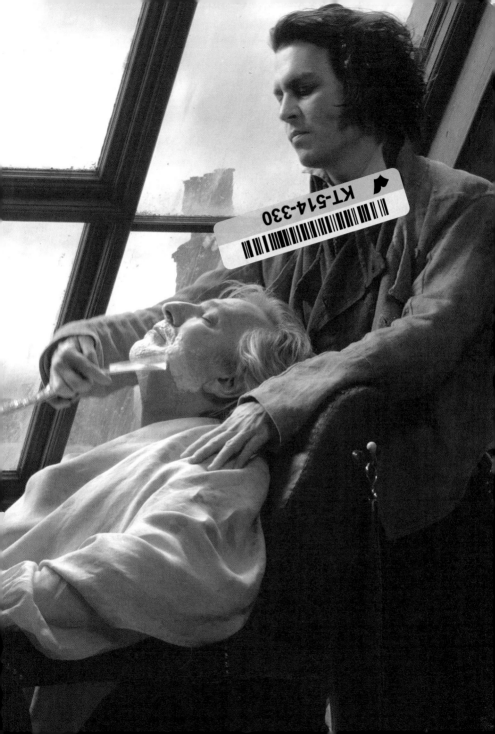

MOVIE ★ ICONS

J. DEPP

EDITOR
PAUL DUNCAN

TEXT
F. X. FEENEY

PHOTOS
THE KOBAL COLLECTION

CONTENTS

1

JOHNNY DEPP: OUTSIDER

BY F. X. FEENEY

JOHNNY DEPP: DER AUSSENSEITER

JOHNNY DEPP: LE MARGINAL

JOHNNY DEPP: OUTSIDER

by F. X. Feeney

Societies are saved by their outsiders. This is the theme of most mythology, with all its misfit heroes, as well as of most John Ford movies, particularly *The Searchers* (1956). One can argue that it is also the theme propelling Johnny Depp's characters.

How do we even describe the alienated beauty of Edward Scissorhands, Ed Wood, Ichabod Crane in *Sleepy Hollow* (1999), Donnie Brasco, Don Juan DeMarco, Captain Jack Sparrow, and Sweeney Todd, apart from Depp? How might we even name them in one sentence, except under the heading of his prodigious, rebellious gift? Only he and his contrary, heat-seeking curiosity and imagination make this unity possible. Otherwise, you would need at least six other actors to achieve what he has thus far in his career.

Acting was something John Christopher Depp backed into. Kentucky-born, Florida-raised Depp first wanted to be a musician. This goal brought him to Los Angeles, but his good looks and physical grace got him noticed, and a friend, actor Nicolas Cage, set up the meeting that led Depp to his first film roles. Shortly he had a hit TV series— *21 Jump Street*—and a fan base of female teenagers he could have exploited toward a very conventional career. He chose to rebel, mocking the whole charade of "celebrity" with his starring role in John Waters' *Cry-Baby* (1990) as a rock 'n' roller torn between his hyperactive tear ducts and criminal impulses. He sealed his image as an eccentric with his next film, Tim Burton's *Edward Scissorhands* (1990), where he deliberately eclipsed his "commercial" face under a mask so alien that *only* a spiritual beauty could come through.

PORTRAIT FOR '21 JUMP STREET' (1987–1990)
This 1950s-style glamour shot gives no clue to the wild, funny, prodigious talent lurking under the skull of its subject. / Diese Glamouraufnahme im Stil der 1950er-Jahre lässt noch nichts ahnen vom wunderbaren, wilden, witzigen Talent, das hinter der Stirn des Porträtierten lauert. / Ce portrait glamour façon années cinquante ne donne aucune idée du prodigieux talent ni de la fantaisie débridée qui se cachent derrière ce joli minois.

"The characters I've played that I've responded to, there has been a lost-soul quality to them."
Johnny Depp

Depp passed this demanding self-test in characteristic style. *Edward Scissorhands* also revealed an important gift in Depp that might otherwise have gone long unnoticed, which is that he *moves* wonderfully. This is a vital quality in any actor, but Depp has been blessed at a level worthy of comparison to Charlie Chaplin and Gary Cooper. After *Benny & Joon* (1993) and *Don Juan DeMarco* (1994), Depp's admirers became all the more plentiful and varied. Critic Elizabeth Pincus once joked in the *L. A. Weekly* that she was the leader of a club called Lesbians in Love with Johnny Depp. (Check out his two cameo appearances in *Before Night Falls* [2000], if you doubt his potential as a gorgeous woman, or what a great Che Guevara he'd have made, in another movie.) Few actors this side of Cary Grant are so angelically androgynous *and* masculine in the same breath.

For a time in the mid-1990s, Depp suffered a crisis in relation to his gift and the cruel chances that unwieldy fame imposed. His friend River Phoenix, a fellow actor of comparable range, died young (through no fault of Depp's) on the sidewalk outside Depp's music club, The Viper Room. Within the next year, as if punishing himself, Depp was twice in trouble with the law—once for trashing a hotel room, once for a disputed accusation of assault. "I didn't understand any of it," he later admitted, of fighting early success. "There was no purpose to it."

He reconnected with his purpose in several ways. One was by directing *The Brave* (1997), a debut that more than lives up to its title by drawing out of costar Marlon Brando a performance that, while brief, is as soul-baring as anything in *Last Tango in Paris* (1972). Depp also recovered his artistic faith by befriending Brando and another longtime hero, Hunter S. Thompson (whom he portrayed in *Fear and Loathing in Las Vegas* [1998]), and drawing deep strength from the examples of their independent spirits. (He most consciously honors these men with his 2004 performance in *The Libertine*.) His third and most life-giving renewal came through love with actress and singer Vanessa Paradis, and, through her, becoming a father in 1999 and 2002.

The depth of his transformation can be seen in his work. The *Pirates of the Caribbean* series (2003–2007) is nothing if not a set of family-friendly features. Taken together, and however tragic their heroes, *The Libertine*, *Finding Neverland* (2004), and *Sweeney Todd* (2007) bespeak the moral core of an outsider determined to make his home in this world, whatever the price.

JOHNNY DEPP: DER AUSSENSEITER

von F. X. Feeney

Eine Gesellschaft wird von ihren Außenseitern gerettet: Das ist der Stoff, aus dem die meisten Heldensagen mit all ihren unkonventionellen Heroen gestrickt sind, aber auch die meisten John-Ford-Filme, insbesondere *Der schwarze Falke* (1956). Man könnte behaupten, dass dies auch das durchgängige Thema von Johnny Depps Charakteren ist.

Wie kann man die entfremdete Schönheit von Edward mit den Scherenhänden, Ed Wood, Ichabod Crane in *Sleepy Hollow* (1999), Donnie Brasco, Don Juan DeMarco, Käpt'n Jack Sparrow und Sweeney Todd ohne Johnny Depp beschreiben? Wie kann man sie überhaupt auf einen Nenner bringen, wenn nicht unter der Rubrik seiner wundersamen, rebellischen Begabung? Nur er und seine gegensätzliche, wärmesuchende Neugier und Vorstellungskraft machen diese Einheit überhaupt möglich. Ohne ihn benötigte man mindestens sechs andere Schauspieler, um das zu schaffen, was er bisher in seiner Karriere erreicht hat.

Zur Schauspielerei kam John Christopher Depp nicht auf direktem Weg. In Kentucky geboren und in Florida aufgewachsen, wollte Depp zunächst Musiker werden. Dieses Ziel brachte ihn nach Los Angeles, aber sein gutes Aussehen erweckte Aufmerksamkeit, und ein Freund – der Schauspieler Nicolas Cage – arrangierte ein Treffen, das Depp zu seinen ersten Filmrollen verhalf. Bald darauf war er in einer erfolgreichen Fernsehserie zu sehen – *21 Jump Street* – und von einer Fangemeinde weiblicher Teenager umlagert. Anstatt darauf jedoch eine konventionelle Karriere aufzubauen, entschied er sich für die Rebellion und verhöhnte das ganze Affentheater um „Ruhm" und „Prominenz" in John Waters' *Cry-Baby* (1990) mit seiner Hauptrolle als Rock 'n' Roller, der zwischen seinen hyperaktiven Tränen-

STILL FROM 'CRY-BABY' (1990)
Television tried to prepackage him, but from his first film Depp carefully chose roles that defied expectation. / Das Fernsehen versuchte, ihn in eine Schublade zu stecken, doch von seinem Filmdebüt an wählte Depp sehr sorgfältig Rollen aus, die nicht den Erwartungen entsprachen. / Bien que la télévision ait tenté de le formater, Johnny Depp choisit dès son premier film des rôles qui défient les attentes.

„Die Charaktere, die ich gespielt habe und die mich ansprachen, könnte man schon in gewisser Weise als verlorene Seelen bezeichnen."
Johnny Depp

drüsen und seinen kriminellen Impulsen hin- und hergerissen ist. Er besiegelte sein Image als Exzentriker dann endgültig mit seinem nächsten Film, Tim Burtons *Edward mit den Scherenhänden* (1990), in dem er sein „gut verkäufliches" Gesicht unter einer so fremdartigen Maske verbarg, dass *nur* seine innere Schönheit zum Tragen kommen konnte.

Depp bestand diesen anspruchsvollen Selbstversuch mit typischer Bravour. *Edward mit den Scherenhänden* brachte auch eine wichtige Begabung Depps an den Tag: Er kann sich wunderbar *bewegen*. Für jeden Schauspieler ist dies eine grundlegende Eigenschaft, doch Depp ist mit einem Talent gesegnet, das sich durchaus an dem von Charlie Chaplin und Gary Cooper messen lassen kann. Nach *Benny und Joon* (1993) und *Don Juan DeMarco* (1994) wuchsen Anzahl und Vielfalt seiner Bewunderer noch weiter. Die Kritikerin Elizabeth Pincus witzelte einst im *L. A. Weekly*, sie sei die Vorsitzende eines Vereins namens „Lesben, die in Johnny Depp verliebt sind". (Man schaue sich nur seine beiden Cameo-Auftritte in *Before Night Falls* [2000] an, falls irgendwelche Zweifel hinsichtlich seines Potenzials als hinreißende Dame bestehen – oder in einem anderen Film, welch einen großartigen „Che" Guevara er abgegeben hätte.) Seit Cary Grant gab es nur wenige Schauspieler, die so engelhaft androgyn und zugleich maskulin sind, wie er.

Eine Zeit lang steckte Depp Mitte der Neunzigerjahre in einer Krise hinsichtlich seiner Begabung und der Folgen eines Ruhms, die er nicht in den Griff bekam. Sein Freund River Phoenix, ein Schauspieler mit vergleichbarem Talent, starb vor Depps Nachtklub, dem „Viper Room" (ohne Depps Zutun). Im Laufe des nächsten Jahres geriet Depp – als wolle er sich selbst bestrafen – zweimal mit dem Gesetz in Konflikt: einmal für die Zerstörung einer Hotelzimmereinrichtung und einmal aufgrund eines tätlichen Angriffs, den er jedoch bestritt. „Ich konnte das überhaupt nicht verstehen", meinte er später über seinen Widerstand gegen den frühen Erfolg. „Es machte keinen Sinn."

Den Sinn fand er auf verschiedenen Wegen wieder. Zum einen inszenierte er sein Filmdebüt *The Brave* (1997), das seinem Titel mehr als gerecht wird, weil es Marlon Brando eine – wenn auch kurze – schauspielerische Leistung entlockt, die mindestens so offenherzig ist wie jede beliebige Szene in *Der letzte Tango in Paris* (1972). Depp fand auch den Glauben an seine Kunst wieder, indem er Freundschaften mit Brando und einem weiteren Idol schloss: Hunter S. Thompson, den er später in *Fear and Loathing in Las Vegas* (1998) auch darstellte. Aus deren unabhängiger Gesinnung schöpfte er eigene Kraft (und er erweist beiden durch seine Rolle in *The Libertine* [2004] bewusster denn je seine Ehre). Seine dritte und erquickendste Erneuerung erlebte er durch seine Liebe zur Schauspielerin und Sängerin Vanessa Paradis und durch die Geburt seiner Kinder 1999 und 2002.

Die Tiefe seiner Wandlung spiegelt sich in seiner Arbeit. Die Reihe *Pirates of the Caribbean* (2003–2007) ist eindeutig eine familienfreundliche Maßnahme. Zusammengenommen – unabhängig von der Tragik ihrer Helden – zeugen *The Libertine*, *Wenn Träume fliegen lernen* (2004) und *Sweeney Todd: Der teuflische Barbier aus der Fleet Street* (2007) vom moralischen Kern eines Außenseiters, der entschlossen ist, sich in dieser Welt ein Zuhause einzurichten – koste es, was es wolle.

STILL FROM 'ED WOOD' (1994)

JOHNNY DEPP : LE MARGINAL

F. X. Feeney

Chaque civilisation doit son salut à des êtres situés en marge de la société. C'est l'idée qui sous-tend la plupart des mythes, avec leurs héros inadaptés à leur milieu, et que l'on retrouve dans les films de John Ford, comme *La Prisonnière du désert* (1956). C'est également l'idée qui anime les personnages incarnés par Johnny Depp.

Comment décrire la beauté décalée d'Edward aux mains d'argent, d'Ed Wood, d'Ichabod Crane dans *Sleepy Hollow* (1999), de Donnie Brasco, de Don Juan DeMarco, du capitaine Jack Sparrow et de Sweeney Todd, sinon en prononçant ce nom : Johnny Depp ? Comment les résumer en une seule phrase, sinon en évoquant son prodigieux talent ? Lui seul, avec son indomptable curiosité et son imagination farouche, est capable de réaliser une telle synthèse. Sans lui, il faudrait au moins six acteurs pour réaliser ce qu'il a accompli depuis le début de sa carrière.

Et pourtant, c'est à reculons que John Christopher Depp est entré dans le métier d'acteur. Né dans le Kentucky, élevé en Floride, le jeune homme veut d'abord être musicien. Cette ambition le conduit jusqu'à Los Angeles, où son physique avantageux et sa grâce naturelle ne passent pas inaperçus. Un ami, l'acteur Nicolas Cage, organise un rendez-vous qui vaudra au jeune Johnny ses premiers rôles au cinéma. Il ne tarde pas à tenir la vedette d'une série télévisée, *21 Jump Street*, et à devenir l'idole d'une foule d'adolescentes. Au lieu d'en profiter pour bâtir une carrière conventionnelle, il opte pour la rébellion. Dans *Cry-Baby* (1990) de John Waters, il tourne en dérision le culte de la célébrité en incarnant un rocker tiraillé entre ses glandes lacrymales et ses pulsions criminelles. Il confirme son image d'excentrique avec le film suivant, *Edward aux mains d'argent* (1990) de Tim Burton, où il éclipse délibérément son visage « commercial » sous un masque si insolite qu'il ne saurait laisser filtrer qu'une beauté spirituelle.

Depp surmonte cette épreuve de vérité avec son panache habituel. *Edward aux mains d'argent* révèle également chez lui un don qui aurait longtemps pu passer inaperçu,

STILL FROM 'SECRET WINDOW' (2004)
John Wayne's famous statement, "I don't act—I react," applies to Depp at his best. / John Waynes berühmter Satz „Ich agiere nicht – ich reagiere" trifft auch auf Depp in seiner Bestform zu. / La célèbre formule de John Wayne, « Je n'agis pas, je réagis », s'applique à Depp dans ses meilleurs moments.

« Les personnages dans lesquels je me suis reconnu ont toujours été des âmes en peine. »
Johnny Depp

son extraordinaire façon de se mouvoir. Une qualité essentielle chez un acteur, mais que Johnny Depp possède à un degré suffisant pour être comparé à Charlie Chaplin ou à Gary Cooper. Après *Benny & Joon* (1993) et *Don Juan DeMarco* (1994), la foule de ses admirateurs devient encore plus dense et plus variée. La critique Elizabeth Pincus déclare avec humour dans le *L. A. Weekly* qu'elle préside le «club des lesbiennes amoureuses de Johnny Depp». (Ses deux brèves apparitions dans *Avant la nuit* [2000] vous convaincront, si besoin est, qu'il serait magnifique en femme... ou en Che Guevara.) Depuis Cary Grant, rares sont les acteurs capables d'être à la fois si innocemment androgynes et si résolument masculins.

Au milieu des années 1990, Johnny Depp traverse une période de crise, incapable d'assumer son talent face à la cruelle loterie imposée par le fardeau de la célébrité. Son ami River Phoenix, acteur d'envergure comparable à la sienne, meurt prématurément devant The Viper Room, le night-club de Johnny Depp (qui n'y est pourtant pour rien). Comme pour se punir, l'acteur a par deux fois affaire à la justice au cours de l'année qui suit : la première pour le saccage d'une chambre d'hôtel, la seconde pour une accusation d'agression qu'il conteste. «Je n'y comprenais rien», confiera-t-il plus tard pour expliquer son refus du succès. «Cela n'avait aucun sens.»

Différents événements l'aideront à redonner un sens à sa carrière. Le premier consistera à faire ses débuts derrière la caméra avec *The Brave* (1997), œuvre courageuse dans laquelle il obtient de son partenaire, Marlon Brando, une prestation qui, malgré sa brièveté, est d'une sincérité digne du *Dernier Tango à Paris* (1972). Depp retrouve également sa foi artistique en se liant d'amitié avec Brando et avec un autre de ses héros de longue date, l'écrivain Hunter S. Thompson (qu'il incarne en 1998 dans *Las Vegas Parano*). Il puisera une immense force dans l'exemple de ces deux esprits indépendants (auxquels il rendra délibérément hommage en 2004 dans *Rochester, le dernier des libertins*). Le troisième et le plus régénérant de ces événements est la rencontre avec la chanteuse et comédienne Vanessa Paradis, avec laquelle il accédera à la paternité en 1999 et 2002.

La profondeur de sa transformation se reflète dans son œuvre. La série des *Pirates des Caraïbes* (2003-2007) possède tous les ingrédients d'un divertissement familial. Pris dans leur ensemble, et aussi tragique que soit le destin de leurs héros, *Rochester, le dernier des libertins*, *Neverland* (2004) et *Sweeney Todd* (2007) témoignent de la rigueur morale d'un marginal déterminé à se forger une place dans ce monde, quel qu'en soit le prix.

PAGE 22
PORTRAIT FOR 'CRY-BABY' (1990)
Depp would not allow himself to be groomed as a conventional "teen idol." He and director John Waters exploded that idea. / Depp ließ sich nicht zum herkömmlichen „Teenagerschwarm" aufbauen: Mit Regisseur John Waters ließ er diese Vorstellung rasch platzen. / Depp, qui refuse de se laisser transformer en «idole des jeunes», tord le cou à cette image avec le réalisateur John Waters.

STILL FROM 'SWEENEY TODD: THE DEMON BARBER OF FLEET STREET' (2007)

2

VISUAL FILMOGRAPHY

FILMOGRAFIE IN BILDERN

FILMOGRAPHIE EN IMAGES

**STILL FROM 'A NIGHTMARE ON ELM STREET'
(1984)**
Prior to his success in television, young Depp navigated
the world of low-budget films, most notably under the
direction of Wes Craven. / Vor seinem Erfolg im
Fernsehen spielte der junge Depp in einigen Billig-
produktionen mit, vor allem für Kultregisseur Wes
Craven. / Avant son succès à la télévision, le jeune
Johnny évolue dans l'univers des séries B, notamment
sous la direction de Wes Craven.

POSTER FOR 'PRIVATE RESORT' (1985)
That is young Mr. Depp, smiling dead center, in the
yellow swimming trunks. / Breit grinsend in der Mitte,
sonnt sich der junge Herr Depp in seiner gelben
Badehose. / Le sieur Johnny Depp trône au beau milieu,
tout sourire dans son caleçon de bain jaune.

PAGES 26/27
STILL FROM 'PLATOON' (1986)
Despite being just another face in the crowd, Depp
(right) got his first ambitious role as an actor from
director Oliver Stone. / Obwohl er hier nur ein weiteres
Gesicht in der Menge war, bekam Depp (rechts) von
Regisseur Oliver Stone immerhin seine erste
anspruchsvolle Rolle. / Bien que noyé dans la foule,
Depp (à droite) obtient son premier rôle ambitieux
auprès du réalisateur Oliver Stone.

PORTRAIT FOR '21 JUMP STREET' (1987–1990)
The widespread buzz about Depp at this early stage in his career was that "He has Sal Mineo's looks, and James Dean's charisma." / In diesem frühen Stadium seiner Karriere erzählte man sich von Depp, er besitze „das Aussehen von Sal Mineo und das Charisma von James Dean". / La réputation qui poursuit Depp au tout début de sa carrière est qu'il a « le physique de Sal Mineo et le charisme de James Dean ».

PORTRAIT FOR '21 JUMP STREET' (1987–1990)
As soon as the TV series lost its social message, Depp (left) lost interest. Note the bored look on Depp's face. / Als die Fernsehserie ihre gesellschaftsrelevante Aussage verlor, verlor Depp (links) das Interesse. Man beachte seinen gelangweilten Gesichtsausdruck. / Une fois dépouillée de son message social, la série télévisée cesse d'intéresser Johnny Depp (à gauche), comme le prouve son air absent.

PORTRAIT FOR 'CRY-BABY' (1990)
Wade "Cry-Baby" Walker (Depp) with fellow "Drapes," played by Traci Lords (center) and Ricki Lake (right). Depp's own humor, and his sincere enjoyment of pop iconography, made for an excellent collaboration between himself and Waters. / Wade „Cry-Baby" Walker (Depp) mit anderen „Drapes", dargestellt unter anderem von Traci Lords (Mitte) und Ricki Lake (rechts). Die Zusammenarbeit mit Waters verlief ausgezeichnet, dank Depps Sinn für Humor und seiner aufrichtigen Begeisterung für die Ikonografie der Popkultur. / Wade Walker alias Cry-Baby (Depp) en compagnie d'autres membres du gang des Drapes, interprétés par Traci Lords (au centre) et Ricki Lake (à droite). Grâce à son humour et à son goût pour l'iconographie pop, l'acteur s'entend à merveille avec John Waters.

PORTRAIT FOR 'CRY-BABY' (1990)
Director Waters specializes in campy parody of iconic pop-culture images. / Regisseur Waters war Spezialist für schnulzige Parodien auf Kultbilder aus der Popkultur. / Le réalisateur John Waters est spécialisé dans les parodies « à l'eau de rose » de la culture pop.

STILL FROM 'CRY-BABY' (1990)
As Wade "Cry-Baby" Walker, Depp gets to sing, fall in
love with Allison (Amy Locane), and be a menace to
polite society. How could Depp say no to this role? /
Als Wade „Cry-Baby" Walker darf Depp singen, sich in
Allison (Amy Locane) verlieben und der vornehmen
Gesellschaft das Fürchten lehren. Wie hätte Depp
diese Rolle ablehnen können? / Comment Depp aurait-il
pu refuser un rôle où il chante, tombe amoureux
d'Allison (Amy Locane) et devient une menace pour
la société bien pensante ?

*"There are people who thought Cry-Baby was a
bad idea, but I've always admired John Waters,
who's never compromised. The easy way is boring
to me."*
Johnny Depp

*„Es gab Leute, die Cry-Baby für einen schlechten
Einfall hielten, aber ich habe John Waters,
der nie Kompromisse einging, stets bewundert.
Der einfache Weg langweilt mich immer."*
Johnny Depp

*« Certains ont estimé que je faisais une erreur en
tournant Cry-Baby, mais j'ai toujours admiré John
Waters, qui n'a jamais fait de concessions. Les
solutions de facilité m'ennuient. »*
Johnny Depp

STILL FROM 'CRY-BABY' (1990)
"Cry-Baby" sheds a tear as he is dragged to jail, away
from the love of his life. / „Cry-Baby" vergießt wieder
mal eine Träne, als man ihn ins Gefängnis schleppt und
damit der Liebe seines Lebens entreißt. / Cry-Baby
verse une larme au moment d'être traîné en prison et
arraché à l'amour de sa vie.

STILL FROM 'EDWARD SCISSORHANDS' (1990)
Acting opposite Vincent Price, the classic interpreter of Edgar Allan Poe, in his last film role. / Mit Vincent Price, dem klassischen Darsteller von Figuren aus der Feder von Edgar Allan Poe, der hier seine letzte Filmrolle spielte. / Avec Vincent Price, le grand interprète d'Edgar Allan Poe, dans son dernier rôle au cinéma.

PORTRAIT FOR 'EDWARD SCISSORHANDS' (1990)
Depp's second outing as a film star, in partnership with director Tim Burton, made clear that the actor was going his own eccentric way. / Depps zweiter Auftritt als Filmstar, diesmal unter der Regie von Tim Burton, machte deutlich, dass der Schauspieler seine eigenen exzentrischen Wege gehen würde. / Le deuxième grand rôle de Johnny Depp au cinéma, en partenariat avec le réalisateur Tim Burton, confirme sa volonté de sortir des sentiers battus.

PAGE 36
STILL FROM 'EDWARD SCISSORHANDS' (1990)
Long an admirer of Charlie Chaplin and Buster Keaton, Depp (with Dianne Wiest) brought a grace of pantomime to shy Edward. / Als langjähriger Bewunderer von Charlie Chaplin und Buster Keaton verlieh Depp (mit Dianne Wiest) der Pantomime des schüchternen Edward eine besondere Anmut. / Fan de Chaplin et de Keaton, Depp (ici aux côtés de Dianne Wiest) apporte une gracieuse touche de pantomime au timide personnage d'Edward.

STILL FROM 'EDWARD SCISSORHANDS' (1990)

Freakish looks and intensity aside, Edward's scissory fingers define him as an artist—his one reliable connection to other human beings. / Abgesehen von seinem ausgefallenen Äußeren und seiner Gefühlstiefe erweist sich Edward durch seine Scherenschnittfiguren als Künstler - seine einzige zuverlässige Verbindung zum Rest der Menschheit. / Abstraction faite de son allure insolite et de son air grave, ses mains en forme de ciseaux font d'Edward un artiste, son seul véritable lien avec le reste de l'humanité.

PAGE 37
PORTRAIT FOR 'EDWARD SCISSORHANDS' (1990)

Depp and Winona Ryder were deeply in love when they made this film together. / Depp und Winona Ryder waren heftig ineinander verliebt, als sie diesen Film drehten. / Johnny Depp et Winona Ryder sont profondément amoureux lors du tournage de ce film.

"I loved playing Edward Scissorhands because there's nothing cynical, jaded, or impure about him. It's almost a letdown to look in the mirror and realize I'm not Edward."
Johnny Depp

„Ich liebte es, Edward mit den Scherenhänden zu spielen, weil es an ihm nichts Zynisches, Reizloses oder Unreines gibt. Es ist beinahe eine Enttäuschung, wenn ich in den Spiegel schaue und feststellen muss, dass ich nicht Edward bin."
Johnny Depp

« J'ai adoré jouer Edward aux mains d'argent, car il n'y a rien de cynique, de blasé ou d'impur en lui. C'est presque une déception de me regarder dans le miroir et de réaliser que je ne suis pas Edward. »
Johnny Depp

STILL FROM 'EDWARD SCISSORHANDS' (1990)
Edward's passionate ice sculptures generate the
romantic snowfall that forms the culminating poetic
image of the film. / Edwards leidenschaftliche
Eisskulpturen erzeugen den romantischen Schneefall,
der den poetischen visuellen Höhepunkt des Films
bildet. / La fougue avec laquelle Edward sculpte la glace
déclenche une superbe «chute de neige», image
poétique qui marque le point culminant du film.

PAGES 40/41
STILL FROM 'EDWARD SCISSORHANDS' (1990)
He has a godlike ability to sculpt animals out of
garden shrubbery, but note his largest fantasy creation—
a normal human hand. / Er besitzt die gottgleiche
Fähigkeit, aus gewöhnlichen Büschen und Sträuchern
Tiere zu schneiden, doch sein größter Wunschtraum
ist - eine gewöhnliche Menschenhand. / Malgré sa
faculté divine à tailler les arbustes en forme d'animaux,
sa plus grande création est une simple main humaine.

STILL FROM 'ARIZONA DREAM' (1993)
Side by side with Faye Dunaway, amid a raucous love
affair in this madcap adventure. / Seite an Seite mit
Faye Dunaway inmitten einer turbulenten Liebes-
geschichte in einem völlig verrückten Abenteuer. /
Aux côtés de Faye Dunaway, avec laquelle il vit une
liaison tumultueuse dans cette aventure échevelée.

*"When I see someone who just follows their dream
and succeeds, and just does basically what they
want to do and doesn't have to answer to anyone,
obviously not harming anyone, that's great."*
Johnny Depp

„*Wenn ich jemanden sehe, der nur seinem Traum
nachgeht und Erfolg hat und im Grunde das tut,
was er tun will, und niemandem Rechenschaft
darüber schuldig ist und natürlich auch niemandem
damit wehtut, dann ist das großartig.*"
Johnny Depp

« *Quand je vois quelqu'un poursuivre ses rêves et
réussir, faire simplement ce qu'il veut sans rendre
de comptes ni nuire à qui que ce soit, je trouve ça
génial.* »
Johnny Depp

STILL FROM 'ARIZONA DREAM' (1993)
This flying machine is a fine metaphor for the film as a
whole—a great, gravity-defying comic epic, directed by
Emir Kusturica. / Dieses Fluggerät ist eine hübsche
Metapher für den Film an sich: ein großartiges und
völlig abgehobenes komisches Epos unter der Regie
von Emir Kusturica. / Son engin volant est une parfaite
métaphore du film : une grande épopée comique
défiant les lois de la gravité, mise en scène par Emir
Kusturica.

STILL FROM 'BENNY & JOON' (1993)
"The dance of the rolls"—a direct homage to Charlie Chaplin, wearing Buster Keaton's trademark hat, opposite Mary Stuart Masterson as Joon. / Neben Mary Stuart Masterson als Joon führt Sam (Depp) den „Brötchentanz" auf - eine unverblümte Hommage an Charlie Chaplin, und dazu mit Hut, Buster Keatons Markenzeichen. / « La danse des petits pains », hommage direct à Charlie Chaplin, avec le chapeau de Buster Keaton et Mary Stuart Masterson dans le rôle de Joon.

PORTRAIT FOR 'BENNY & JOON' (1993)
Depp prepared for this role by putting in long hours at the renowned Silent Movie Theatre in Los Angeles. / Depp bereitete sich auf diese Rolle vor, indem er viele Stunden im berühmten Stummfilmkino von Los Angeles verbrachte. / Afin de se préparer pour ce rôle, Depp passe de longues heures au Silent Movie Theatre, cinéma de Los Angeles spécialisé dans les films muets.

STILL FROM 'BENNY & JOON' (1993)
Looking very much the silent-film star. / Hier erinnert er
besonders stark an den Stummfilmstar. / Tout droit sorti
d'un film muet.

STILL FROM 'BENNY & JOON' (1993)
The poignancy of this film grows out of his loving efforts
to cheer Joon away from her afflicted tendency to
suicidal despair. / Der Film bezieht seine Melancholie
aus den liebenswerten Bemühungen, Joon durch
Aufmunterung von ihrer krankhaften Neigung zu
selbstzerstörerischer Verzweiflung zu befreien. / Ce qui
rend ce film poignant, c'est la tendresse avec laquelle
Benny s'efforce de distraire Joon de ses démons et de
ses angoisses suicidaires.

STILL FROM 'WHAT'S EATING GILBERT GRAPE?' (1993)

Gilbert Grape (Depp, here kissing Mary Steenburgen) is overwhelmed by unfair responsibilities, and desperate to seize his diminishing chances in life. / Gilbert Grape (Depp, der hier Mary Steenburgen küsst) wird von der Verantwortung überwältigt, die man ihm unfairerweise aufgebürdet hat, und versucht verzweifelt, seine schwindenden Chancen im Leben zu nutzen. / Accablé par de trop lourdes responsabilités, Gilbert Grape (Depp, qui embrasse ici Mary Steenburgen) tente désespérément de saisir les chances que lui offre encore la vie.

STILL FROM 'WHAT'S EATING GILBERT GRAPE?' (1993)

Among Gilbert's more frustrating burdens is his sweet but mentally retarded brother Arnie (Leonardo DiCaprio). / Zu Gilberts frustrierenden Bürden gehört sein liebenswürdiger, aber geistig zurückgebliebener Bruder Arnie (Leonardo DiCaprio). / Parmi les fardeaux qui pèsent sur Gilbert se trouve son petit frère Arnie (Leonardo DiCaprio), un garçon attachant mais retardé.

PAGES 50/51
STILL FROM 'WHAT'S EATING GILBERT GRAPE?' (1993)

Leonardo DiCaprio made such a powerful debut that he was nominated for an Oscar. / Leonardo DiCaprios Kino-Debüt trug ihm gleich eine „Oscar"-Nominierung ein. / En guise de coup d'essai, Leonardo DiCaprio signe un coup de maître et est sélectionné pour les Oscars.

STILL FROM 'WHAT'S EATING GILBERT GRAPE?' (1993)
"You are my knight in shimmering armor," Gilbert's despondent mother, Bonnie (Darlene Cates), tells him at a decisive moment. / „Du bist mein Ritter in schimmernder Rüstung", gesteht Gilberts mutlos gewordene Mutter Bonnie (Darlene Cates) ihrem Sohn in einem entscheidenden Augenblick. / Désemparée, Bonnie (Darlene Cates), la mère de Gilbert, lui confie à cet instant décisif : « Tu es mon brillant chevalier. »

STILL FROM 'WHAT'S EATING GILBERT GRAPE?' (1993)
Love with Becky (Juliette Lewis) keeps Gilbert sane. Directed by Lasse Hallström, this film beautifully dramatizes the nature of dignity. / Durch seine Liebe zu Becky (Juliette Lewis) wahrt Gilbert seinen Verstand. Dieser Film unter der Regie von Lasse Hallström dramatisiert auf wundervolle Weise die Bedeutung von Würde. / Dans ce film de Lasse Hallström qui illustre magnifiquement la quête de la dignité, Gilbert se raccroche à son amour pour Becky (Juliette Lewis) pour ne pas devenir fou.

STILL FROM 'ED WOOD' (1994)
In real life, Edward D. Wood Jr., maestro of cheesy special effects, was dismissed by critics as "the worst film director of all time." / Im wahren Leben wurde Edward D. Wood jr., der Meister billiger Spezialeffekte, von Kritikern als „schlechtester Filmregisseur aller Zeiten" abgetan. / Le véritable Ed Wood, spécialiste des effets kitsch, était considéré par la critique comme « le plus mauvais cinéaste de tous les temps ».

PAGES 54/55
STILL FROM 'ED WOOD' (1994)
Edward D. Wood Jr., filmmaker. A very different Edward from Edward Scissorhands, but no less endearing, as events unfold. / Filmemacher Edward D. Wood jr.: ein ganz anderer Edward als Edward mit den Scherenhänden, der sich jedoch im Laufe der Handlung als kaum weniger liebenswert erweist. / Dans le rôle du cinéaste Edward D. Wood Jr., Johnny Depp campe un « Edward » fort différent mais finalement aussi attachant qu'Edward aux mains d'argent.

"There's a game to be played here [in Hollywood]. You can play it to the hilt and make shit-piles of money. I don't want to be 90 years old and look back and see how full of shit I was. The people I admire didn't do that."
Johnny Depp

STILL FROM 'ED WOOD' (1994)
A lovable loser, he surrounded himself with lost souls of every stripe. (George "The Animal" Steele, Juliet Landau, and Martin Landau.) / Ein liebenswerter Verlierer, der sich mit verlorenen Seelen aller Art umgab (George „The Animal" Steele, Juliet Landau und Martin Landau). / Adorable loser, il s'entoure de paumés en tous genres (George « The Animal » Steele, Juliet Landau et Martin Landau).

„Hier [in Hollywood] gibt es ein Spiel. Man kann es bis zum Äußersten ausreizen und einen Haufen Geld machen. Wenn ich neunzig bin, will ich nicht zurückschauen und sehen, wie viel Scheiße ich gemacht habe. Die Leute, die ich bewundere, haben das nicht gemacht."
Johnny Depp

« On peut jouer gros ici [à Hollywood]. On peut jouer le jeu à fond et se faire un paquet de fric. Mais je ne veux pas regarder en arrière à 90 ans et me rendre compte que j'ai été complètement bidon. Les gens que j'admire n'étaient pas comme ça. »
Johnny Depp

STILL FROM 'ED WOOD' (1994)
Depp, director Tim Burton, and writers Scott Alexander and Larry Karaszewski suggest that Wood's passionate enthusiasm was his saving grace. / Depp, Regisseur Tim Burton und die Autoren Scott Alexander und Larry Karaszewski suggerieren, dass Woods leidenschaftliche Begeisterung seine Rettung war. / Pour Johnny Depp, le réalisateur Tim Burton et les scénaristes Scott Alexander et Larry Karaszewski, ce qui sauve Ed Wood est son enthousiasme passionné.

STILL FROM 'ED WOOD' (1994)
Martin Landau won an Oscar for his role as legendary (but now washed-up) Dracula star Bela Lugosi. / Martin Landau erhielt einen „Oscar" für seine Rolle als legendärer (aber inzwischen abgetakelter) Dracula-Star Bela Lugosi. / Martin Landau remportera un oscar pour le rôle de l'acteur Bela Lugosi, interprète légendaire (mais quelque peu dépassé) du personnage de Dracula.

STILL FROM 'ED WOOD' (1994)
Ed, a cross-dresser, has a greater passion for his date's
angora sweater than for the lady herself (Sarah Jessica
Parker). / Transvestit Ed entwickelt eine größere
Leidenschaft für den Angorapulli der jungen Dame
(Sarah Jessica Parker), mit der er sich verabredet hat,
als für sie selbst. / Travesti dans l'âme, Ed s'intéresse
plus au pull en angora de sa conquête qu'à la jeune
femme elle-même (Sarah Jessica Parker).

STILL FROM 'ED WOOD' (1994)
Revealing his true self. Whatever else one might make
of Ed Wood, he was always forthright about what he
dreamt of becoming. / Er zeigt sein wahres Ich: Man
konnte von Ed Wood halten, was man wollte – er
machte nie einen Hehl daraus, was er einmal werden
wollte. / Ed tel qu'en lui-même. Quoi qu'on pense de lui,
Ed Wood a toujours été franc sur ce qu'il rêvait d'être.

*"I don't pretend to be Captain Weird.
I just do what I do."*
Johnny Depp

*„Ich tu nicht so, als sei ich ‚Kapitän Schräg'.
Ich mache einfach, was ich mache."*
Johnny Depp

*« Je ne fais pas semblant d'être excentrique.
Je suis comme je suis. »*
Johnny Depp

STILL FROM 'DON JUAN DEMARCO' (1995)
Acting opposite Marlon Brando was to prove a defining moment in Depp's life and career. / Die Rolle an der Seite von Marlon Brando erwies sich als prägend für Depps Leben und seine Karriere. / La rencontre avec Marlon Brando sera un moment décisif dans la vie et la carrière de Johnny Depp.

STILL FROM 'DON JUAN DEMARCO' (1995)
This may well be Depp's single most romantic role—a beautiful young man capable of transforming himself into every woman's fantasy. / Dies war möglicherweise Depps romantischste Rolle: ein gut aussehender junger Mann, der sich in die Fantasievorstellung einer jeden Frau verwandeln kann. / Peut-être le rôle le plus romantique de la carrière de Johnny Depp : un beau jeune homme capable d'assouvir les fantasmes de chaque femme.

STILL FROM 'DON JUAN DEMARCO' (1995)
The film abounds in upbeat, sexy fantasy sequences. /
Der Film ist randvoll mit munter-erotischen Fantasie-
sequenzen. / Le film regorge de séquences oniriques
d'un érotisme enjoué.

STILL FROM 'DON JUAN DEMARCO' (1995)
Much as he needs the services of Brando's psycho-
analyst, Depp's DeMarco is able to make his daydreams
come to life. / Wenngleich er die Hilfe eines
Psychoanalytikers (Brando) in Anspruch nimmt, ist
DeMarco (Depp) doch in der Lage, seine Tagträume mit
Leben zu füllen. / Bien qu'il ait besoin des services d'un
psychiatre (Brando), Don Juan DeMarco parvient à
donner vie à ses rêves.

STILL FROM 'DON JUAN DEMARCO' (1995)
A reality more fulfilling than any harem fantasy, kissing Julia (Talisa Soto). / Eine Wirklichkeit, die erfüllender ist als jegliche Haremsfantasie: ein Kuss für Julia (Talisa Soto). / Une réalité plus épanouissante que n'importe quel fantasme érotique dans les bras de Julia (Talisa Soto).

STILL FROM 'DON JUAN DEMARCO' (1995)
DeMarco is a red-blooded romantic of boundless imaginary appetite. / DeMarco ist ein heißblütiger Romantiker mit einem grenzenlosen imaginären Appetit. / DeMarco est un romantique au sang chaud doté d'un appétit et d'une imagination sans limites.

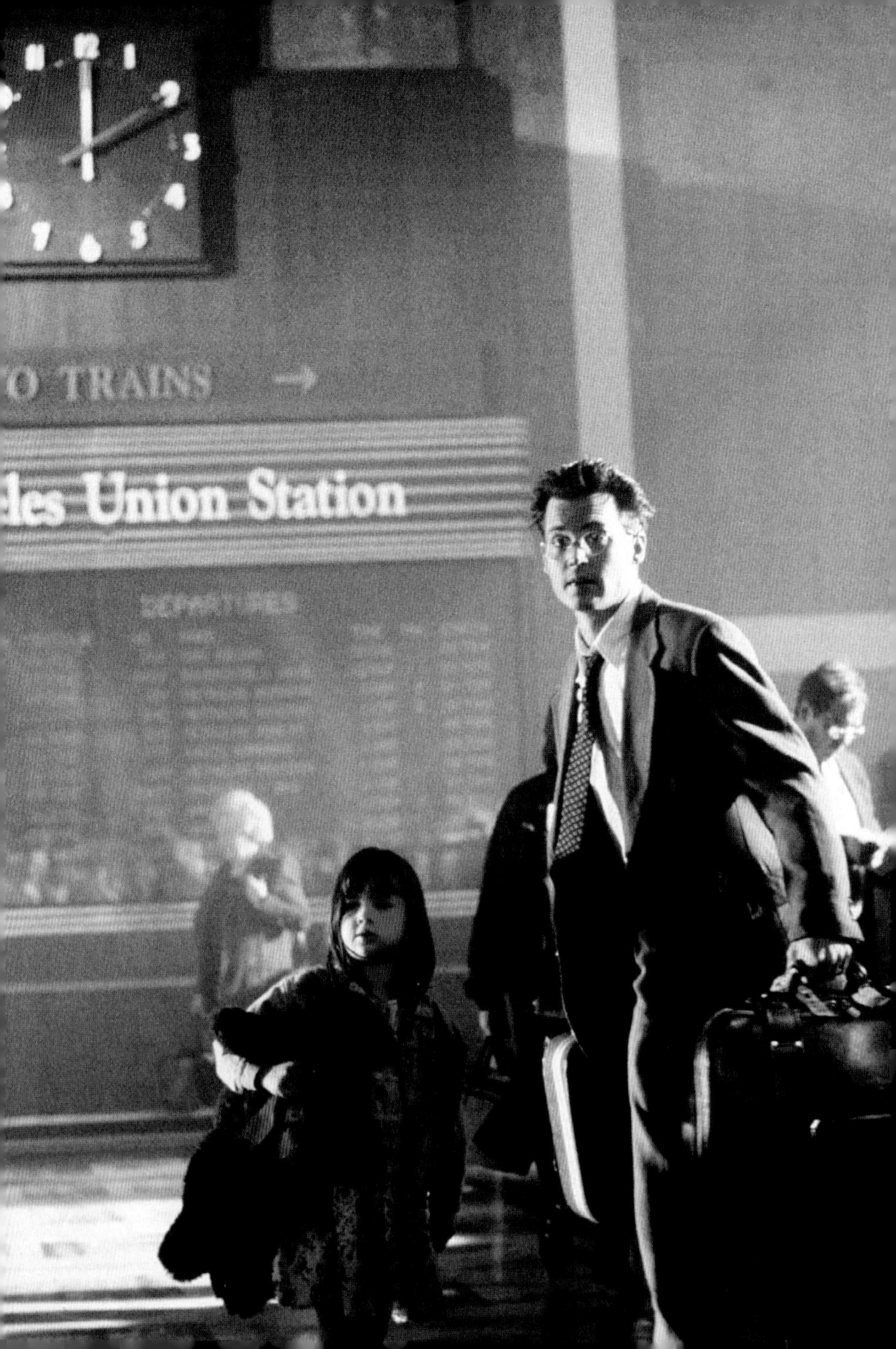
O TRAINS →
eles Union Station

STILL FROM 'NICK OF TIME' (1995)
The classic "innocent man in jeopardy"—Mr. Smith (Christopher Walken) is the menacing thug reflected in Depp's eyeglasses. / Der klassische „Unschuldige in Gefahr" – der bedrohliche Übeltäter, der sich in Depps Brille spiegelt, ist Mr. Smith (Christopher Walken). / Une classique histoire « d'innocent en péril » où la menace vient de M. Smith (Christopher Walken), reflété dans les lunettes de Johnny Depp.

STILL FROM 'NICK OF TIME' (1995)
A traditional thriller, in the Hitchcock manner. Gene Watson (Depp) is an ordinary father eager to protect his daughter (Courtney Chase). / Ein traditioneller Thriller in Hitchcockmanier. Gene Watson (Depp) ist ein gewöhnlicher Vater, der seine Tochter (Courtney Chase) beschützen möchte. / Un thriller traditionnel dans la veine de Hitchcock où Depp incarne Gene Watson, un homme ordinaire soucieux de protéger sa fille (Courtney Chase).

STILL FROM 'NICK OF TIME' (1995)
The film, directed by John Badham, takes place in "real time," over 90 minutes. / Der Film von Regisseur John Badham spielt über 90 Minuten in Echtzeit. / Réalisé par John Badham, ce film se déroule «en temps réel» sur 90 minutes.

STILL FROM 'NICK OF TIME' (1995)
To save his daughter's life, Watson must assassinate Governor Grant (Marsha Mason, right), but instead he makes repeated attempts to warn her. / Um das Leben seiner Tochter zu retten, soll Watson Gouverneur Grant (Marsha Mason, rechts) ermorden, doch stattdessen versucht er wiederholt, sie zu warnen. / Pour sauver sa fille, Watson doit assassiner le gouverneur Grant (Marsha Mason, à droite), mais il tente sans cesse de l'avertir du danger.

STILL FROM 'DEAD MAN' (1995)
Depp plays poetic traveler William Blake, named in honor of the great English poet who wrote 'Songs of Innocence and Experience.' / Depp spielt den poetischen Reisenden William Blake, benannt nach dem großen englischen Dichter, der *Lieder der Unschuld und Erfahrung* schrieb. / Depp entame un voyage poétique dans le rôle de William Blake, ainsi nommé en l'honneur du grand poète anglais, auteur des *Chants d'innocence et d'expérience*.

"Oh, yeah. 'That guy can't open a film. He does all those weird art movies. He works with directors whose names we can't pronounce.' ... But there are worse things you could say."
Johnny Depp

„Oh, ja. ‚Der Kerl kann keinen Film tragen. Er macht all diese sonderbaren Kunstfilme. Er arbeitet mit Regisseuren zusammen, deren Namen wir nicht aussprechen können.' ... Man könnte Schlimmeres über mich sagen."
Johnny Depp

« Oh oui. "Ce mec ne fait pas vendre. Il joue dans des films d'auteur bizarres. Il bosse avec des cinéastes au nom imprononçable." [...] Mais il y a pire, comme critiques. »
Johnny Depp

STILL FROM 'DEAD MAN' (1995)
Innocence and Experience collide when William dallies
with the wrong woman (Mili Avital) and is dispatched on
a dreamlike odyssey. / Unschuld und Erfahrung prallen
auch aufeinander, als sich William mit der falschen Frau
(Mili Avital) einlässt und auf eine traumgleiche Irrfahrt
geschickt wird. / L'innocence et l'expérience se
télescopent lorsque William badine avec la mauvaise
personne (Mili Avital) et se retrouve embarqué dans
une odyssée onirique.

STILL FROM 'DEAD MAN' (1995)
William Blake's unexpected guide, after he wakes
up with a bullet wound, is a highly talkative Native
American (Gary Farmer). / Nachdem William Blake mit
einer Schusswunde aufwacht, wird ein äußerst
geschwätziger Indianer (Gary Farmer) unerwartet zu
seinem Führer. / Lorsqu'il se réveille blessé à la poitrine,
William Blake trouve un guide inattendu en la personne
d'un Indien volubile (Gary Farmer).

PAGES 76/77
STILL FROM 'DEAD MAN' (1995)
Writer/director Jim Jarmusch hints that his hero may be
dreaming a tale as he dies. / Autor und Regisseur Jim
Jarmusch deutet an, dass sein Protagonist die Handlung
nur träumt, als er im Sterben liegt. / Le scénariste et
réalisateur Jim Jarmusch suggère que son héros
agonisant est victime d'un mauvais rêve.

STILL FROM 'DEAD MAN' (1995)
Depp, part Cherokee, is ideal as a misfit whose
hallucinatory journey hints that he is recovering his
real roots. / Depp, der selbst Cherokee-Wurzeln hat,
passt ideal in die Rolle des Außenseiters, dessen
halluzinatorische Reise darauf hindeutet, dass er seine
wahren Wurzeln wiederentdeckt. / Avec ses origines
cherokee, Depp est parfait dans ce rôle de marginal
dont le voyage hallucinatoire vers une réalité plus
profonde et plus folklorique s'apparente à une quête
de ses racines.

STILL FROM 'DONNIE BRASCO' (1997)
Here, Depp (with Anne Heche playing his wife) balances his surrealist inclinations with a multidimensional, psychological portrait of an undercover cop. / Hier gleicht Depp (mit Anne Heche in der Rolle seiner Ehefrau) seine surrealistischen Neigungen durch das facettenreiche psychologische Porträt eines verdeckten Ermittlers aus. / Délaissant ses penchants surréalistes, Johnny Depp (aux côtés d'Anne Heche, qui incarne sa femme) brosse le portrait psychologique complexe d'un policier chargé d'infiltrer la mafia.

STILL FROM 'DONNIE BRASCO' (1997)
The true story of Joseph Pistone, a detective calling himself Donnie Brasco, who infiltrated the innermost circles of organized crime. / Die wahre Geschichte von Joseph Pistone, einem Kripobeamten, der sich Donnie Brasco nannte und bis in die innersten Kreise des organisierten Verbrechens eindrang. / L'histoire véridique de Joseph Pistone, agent du FBI qui se faisait appeler « Donnie Brasco » pour infiltrer les cercles les plus fermés de la mafia.

STILL FROM 'DONNIE BRASCO' (1997)
Donnie's undercover work becomes complicated when
he forms an emotional bond with a low-level gangster,
Ben "Lefty" Ruggiero (Al Pacino). / Donnies verdeckte
Ermittlungen werden kompliziert, als er beginnt, sich
mit dem Kleingangster Ben „Lefty" Ruggiero (Al Pacino)
gut zu verstehen. / La mission clandestine de Donnie se
complique lorsqu'il se lie d'amitié avec un modeste
gangster, Ben Ruggiero alias « Lefty » (Al Pacino).

"All the amazing people that I've worked with—
Marlon Brando, Al Pacino, Dustin Hoffman—have
told me consistently: Don't compromise. Do your
work, and if what you're giving is not what they
want, you have to be prepared to walk away."
Johnny Depp

„All die erstaunlichen Leute, mit denen ich
zusammengearbeitet habe – Marlon Brando,
Al Pacino, Dustin Hoffman –, haben mir
übereinstimmend geraten: ‚Geh keine Kompromisse
ein. Mach deine Arbeit, und wenn das, was du
gibst, nicht das ist, was sie wollen, dann musst du
bereit sein zu gehen."
Johnny Depp

STILL FROM 'DONNIE BRASCO' (1997)
Pacino gives a beautifully layered performance as Lefty,
a defeated and essentially kind-hearted man born to
the world of crime. / Pacino liefert eine wunderbar
vielschichtige schauspielerische Leistung als Lefty, ein
geschlagener, aber im Grunde seines Herzens gütiger
Mensch, der in die Welt des Verbrechens hinein-
geboren wurde. / Al Pacino interprète avec brio
le personnage complexe de Lefty, un homme abattu et
fondamentalement bon né dans un monde de truands.

« Tous les grands acteurs avec qui j'ai travaillé
(Marlon Brando, Al Pacino, Dustin Hoffman) m'ont
toujours dit : Ne fais pas de concessions. Fais ton
boulot, et si ce que tu leur donnes ne leur convient
pas, sois prêt à claquer la porte. »
Johnny Depp

STILL FROM 'THE BRAVE' (1997)
To feed his family, Raphael (Depp) makes a brave but
sinister bargain with a melancholy billionaire (Marlon
Brando). / Um seine Familie zu ernähren, lässt sich
Raphael (Depp) auf ein mutiges, aber dunkles Geschäft
mit einem melancholischen Milliardär (Marlon Brando)
ein. / Pour nourrir sa famille, Raphael (Depp) conclut un
marché courageux mais sinistre avec un mélancolique
milliardaire (Marlon Brando).

STILL FROM 'THE BRAVE' (1997)
Johnny Depp made his debut as a director, drawing on
his Native American heritage. / Johnny Depp gab seinen
Einstand als Regisseur, indem er erneut auf seine
indianische Abstammung zurückgriff. / Pour ses débuts
de réalisateur, Johnny Depp puise dans son héritage
amérindien.

STILL FROM 'FEAR AND LOATHING IN LAS VEGAS' (1998)
Poised for Hunter S. Thompson's classic yarn about a drug-hazed trip through "the savage heart of the American Dream." / In der passenden Pose für Hunter S. Thompsons klassische Geschichte über einen drogenvernebelten Trip durch „das wilde Herz des amerikanischen Traums". / Prêt à entamer un voyage halluciné sur les traces de Hunter S. Thompson à travers « le cœur sauvage du rêve américain ».

"I like the idea of images and sounds that don't necessarily mean story and plot."
Johnny Depp

„Mir gefällt die Vorstellung von Bildern und Tönen, die nicht unbedingt Geschichte und Handlung ergeben."
Johnny Depp

« J'aime l'idée que des images et des sons ne correspondent pas nécessairement à une histoire et à une intrigue. »
Johnny Depp

STILL FROM 'FEAR AND LOATHING IN LAS VEGAS' (1998)
Dr. Gonzo (Benicio Del Toro), the "Samoan" attorney, accompanies Raoul Duke (Depp) into the desert. / Dr. Gonzo (Benicio Del Toro), der „samoanische" Anwalt, begleitet Raoul Duke (Depp) in die Wüste. / Maître Gonzo (Benicio Del Toro), l'avocat « samoan », accompagne Raoul Duke (Depp) dans le désert.

STILL FROM 'FEAR AND LOATHING IN LAS VEGAS' (1998)
Depp lived for a time with the real Hunter S. Thompson while preparing for this role. The two became great friends. / Depp quartierte sich eine Zeit lang bei Hunter S. Thompson ein, während er sich auf diese Rolle vorbereitete. Die beiden wurden zu dicken Freunden. / L'acteur, qui a vécu quelque temps avec Hunter S. Thompson afin de se préparer pour le rôle, est devenu très ami avec lui.

STILL FROM 'THE NINTH GATE' (1999)
The ruthless tactics of Dean Corso (Depp), a dealer in rare books, bring him business from a circle of rather demonic book buyers. / Durch seine skrupellosen Taktiken kommt Dean Corso (Depp), der mit Buchraritäten handelt, mit einem Zirkel reichlich dämonischer Kunden ins Geschäft. / Impitoyable dénicheur de livres rares, Dean Corso (Depp) en vient à travailler pour un cercle d'acheteurs assez démoniaques.

STILL FROM 'THE NINTH GATE' (1999)
One of Corso's fellow booksellers winds up dead, posed like 'The Hanged Man' in a tarot deck. / Einer von Corsos Buchhändlerkollegen zahlt mit dem Leben und endet in der Pose des „Gehängten" aus den Tarotkarten. / L'un des confrères de Corso est retrouvé mort dans la position du pendu d'un jeu de tarot.

PAGES 90/91
STILL FROM 'THE NINTH GATE' (1999)
Roman Polanski masterfully directed this playful film, based on the best-selling 'El club Dumas' by Arturo Pérez-Reverte. / Roman Polanski führte meisterlich Regie bei diesem verspielten Film nach dem Bestseller *Der Club Dumas* von Arturo Pérez-Reverte. / Roman Polanski dirige avec brio ce film ludique inspiré d'un best-seller d'Arturo Pérez-Reverte, *Club Dumas*.

STILL FROM 'THE NINTH GATE' (1999)
A possibly supernatural mystery woman (Emmanuelle Seigner) both taunts and helps Corso. / Eine mysteriöse und möglicherweise übernatürliche Frau (Emmanuelle Seigner) führt Corso in die Irre und hilft ihm zugleich. / Une mystérieuse créature aux pouvoirs apparemment surnaturels (Emmanuelle Seigner) aide Corso tout en se jouant de lui.

STILL FROM 'THE NINTH GATE' (1999)
Corso becomes a detective by default, searching the maze of lethal mysteries that surround a single book. / Corso wird zum Detektiv wider Willen, der ein Labyrinth todbringender Geheimnisse erkunden muss, die sich alle um ein einziges Buch drehen. / Devenu détective malgré lui, Corso explore le dédale de mystères mortifères qui entoure un étrange ouvrage.

STILL FROM 'THE NINTH GATE' (1999)
A book called 'The Nine Gates of the Kingdom of
Shadows' maps a demonic landscape, and here is gate
number nine. / Ein Buch mit dem Titel *De umbrarum
regni novem portis* enthält die Karte zu einer
dämonischen Landschaft, und hier ist die neunte
Pforte. / Un livre intitulé *Les Neuf Portes du Royaume
des Ombres* décrit un paysage diabolique, dont voici
la neuvième porte.

STILL FROM 'THE NINTH GATE' (1999)
In a world of cosmic absurdities, Roman Polanski suggests that love is the devil. For Corso, this notion is literally overwhelming. / In einer Welt kosmischer Absurditäten suggeriert Roman Polanski, dass die Liebe der Teufel ist. Corso ist von dieser Vorstellung buchstäblich überwältigt. / Dans un monde d'absurdité cosmique, Roman Polanski suggère que le diable n'est autre que l'amour, notion littéralement renversante pour Corso.

"I remember carving my initials on my arm and I've scarred myself from time to time since then. In a way your body is a journal and the scars are sort of entries in it."
Johnny Depp

„Ich erinnere mich daran, wie ich mir mal meine Initialen in den Arm ritzte, und ich habe mich seitdem immer mal wieder selbst verletzt. Der Körper ist in gewisser Weise ein Tagebuch, und die Narben sind Einträge darin."
Johnny Depp

« Je me souviens m'être gravé mes initiales dans le bras et depuis, il m'est arrivé de me balafrer. Notre corps est comme un journal intime rempli de cicatrices. »
Johnny Depp

STILL FROM 'THE ASTRONAUT'S WIFE' (1999)
Jillian (Charlize Theron) is married to astronaut
Commander Spencer Armacost (Depp), who has
returned to Earth in a transformed condition. / Jillian
(Charlize Theron) ist mit dem Astronauten Commander
Spencer Armacost (Depp) verheiratet, der verändert
auf die Erde zurückgekehrt ist. / Mariée à l'astronaute
Spencer Armacost (Depp), Jillian (Charlize Theron)
trouve son mari transformé au retour d'une expédition.

*"Marlon [Brando] was a pioneer, so I wouldn't even
put myself in the same thought bubble with him,
but he understood a lot of things about me, and
was incredibly generous and helpful and caring.
Very rarely did we talk about movies or acting, so
it wasn't that. He saw me going through stuff he'd
been through—my weird hillbilly rage—so, yeah, the
connection was strong and deep."*
Johnny Depp

*„Marlon [Brando] war ein Pionier, also würde
ich mich selbst nicht einmal in die gleiche
Gedankenblase setzen wie er - aber er begriff
sehr viele Dinge an mir und war so unglaublich
großzügig und hilfreich und fürsorgend. Wir
sprachen sehr selten über Filme oder Schauspielerei - das war's also nicht. Er sah, wie ich
Sachen durchmachte, die er auch durchgemacht
hatte - meine sonderbaren Wutausbrüche - also,
ja: Die Verbindung war stark und tief.“*
Johnny Depp

STILL FROM 'THE ASTRONAUT'S WIFE' (1999)
One can see what appealed to Depp about this role—a
chance to represent a monstrous personality change,
entirely without makeup. / Man erkennt leicht, was
Depp an dieser Rolle reizte: die Möglichkeit, eine
monströse Persönlichkeitsveränderung ganz ohne
Maske zu spielen. / Enfin un rôle où Johnny Depp peut
se transformer en monstre sans aucun maquillage!

PAGES 98/99
STILL FROM 'SLEEPY HOLLOW' (1999)
Reunited with director Tim Burton, Depp radically
reimagines Washington Irving's classically awkward
18th-century hero, Ichabod Crane. / Wieder unter der
Regie von Tim Burton liefert Depp eine radikal neue
Interpretation von Washington Irvings Ichabod Crane,
dem linkischen Helden aus dem 18. Jahrhundert. / Pour
ses retrouvailles avec Tim Burton, Depp réinvente
entièrement le personnage d'Ichabod Crane, héros
maladroit du XVIIIe siècle créé par Washington Irving.

*« Marlon [Brando] était un pionnier et je n'oserais
jamais me comparer à lui, mais il comprenait
beaucoup de choses à mon sujet et se montrait
incroyablement généreux, serviable et attentionné.
Nous parlions très rarement du cinéma et du
métier d'acteur, il ne s'agissait pas de cela. Il me
voyait confronté à des choses qu'il avait connues,
comme mes accès de rage assez rustre, et nous
avions donc un lien puissant et profond. »*
Johnny Depp

STILL FROM 'SLEEPY HOLLOW' (1999)
In the original tale, Ichabod is a freakish schoolteacher.
Here, he is a handsome detective, armed with gadgets
of his own invention. / In Irvings Erzählung ist Ichabod
ein verschrobener Lehrer, hier hingegen ein gut
aussehender Detektiv, ausgerüstet mit allerlei
technischem Spielzeug, das er selbst erfunden hat. /
Instituteur fantasque dans la nouvelle d'origine, Ichabod
devient un détective au physique agréable armé de
gadgets de son invention.

"Am I a romantic? I've seen Wuthering Heights
10 times. I'm a romantic."
Johnny Depp

„Bin ich ein Romantiker? Ich habe Wuthering
Heights zehnmal gesehen. Ich bin ein Romantiker."
Johnny Depp

« Si je suis romantique ? J'ai vu Les Hauts de
Hurlevent dix fois. Et comment, que je suis
romantique. »
Johnny Depp

STILL FROM 'SLEEPY HOLLOW' (1999)
The beauty in the blindfold is Katrina Van Tassel
(Christina Ricci). / Die Schöne mit den verbundenen
Augen ist Katrina Van Tassel (Christina Ricci). / La belle
aux yeux bandés est Katrina Van Tassel (Christina Ricci).

PAGES 102/103
STILL FROM 'SLEEPY HOLLOW' (1999)
Burton evoked the haunted, frontier atmosphere of
1799 New York by shooting mostly on soundstages. /
Burton ahmte die gespenstische Atmosphäre des 1799
an der Siedlungsgrenze gelegenen Staates New York
nach, indem er hauptsächlich im Studio drehte. / Tim
Burton recrée l'atmosphère rude et inquiétante d'une
bourgade reculée de la Nouvelle-Angleterre en 1799 en
tournant la plupart des scènes en studio.

STILL FROM 'SLEEPY HOLLOW' (1999)
To solve the mysterious deaths in the village of Sleepy
Hollow, Ichabod must first fight the panic of the local
populace. / Um die mysteriösen Todesfälle im Nest
Sleepy Hollow zu klären, muss Ichabod zunächst gegen
die panische Angst der Dorfbewohner ankämpfen. /
Pour élucider les mystérieux meurtres du village de
Sleepy Hollow, Ichabod doit affronter la panique de la
population locale.

*"I started out as a guitarist in the early 1980s.
I hooked up with a guy who idolized James Dean
and he gave me a copy of the Dean biography,
The Mutant King, which I thought was really
interesting. While reading the book I watched
Rebel Without a Cause, and I thought, 'Wow, this
guy really has something,' and I was hooked. I
wasn't really into acting at the time—but James
Dean was the catalyst."*
Johnny Depp

*„Ich fing in den 1980er Jahren als Gitarrist an. Ich
tat mich mit einem Typen zusammen, der James
Dean vergötterte, und er gab mir ein Exemplar
der Dean-Biografie The Mutant King, die ich
wirklich interessant fand. Während ich das Buch
las, schaute ich mir ... denn sie wissen nicht, was
sie tun an, und ich dachte: ‚Wow, dieser Kerl
hat wirklich was!' – und ich war abhängig. Ich
interessierte mich bis dahin nicht wirklich für
die Schauspielerei – aber James Dean war der
Katalysator."*
Johnny Depp

STILL FROM 'SLEEPY HOLLOW' (1999)
The world of the supernatural freely interacts here with
a solidly detailed evocation of early America. / Die Welt
des Übernatürlichen wird hier im freien Wechselspiel
mit einer detailgetreuen Nachbildung der frühen USA
dargestellt. / L'univers surnaturel interagit librement
avec un tableau scrupuleusement détaillé de l'Amérique
des pionniers.

*« J'ai débuté comme guitariste au début des
années 1980. Je connaissais un mec qui idolâtrait
James Dean et qui m'a prêté sa biographie,* James
Dean le rebelle, *que j'ai trouvée passionnante.
Pendant que je la lisais, j'ai vu* La Fureur de vivre ;
*je me suis dit : "Ce mec a vraiment quelque chose",
et j'ai été conquis. Je ne pensais pas devenir acteur
à l'époque, mais James Dean a servi de déclic. »*
Johnny Depp

STILL FROM 'THE MAN WHO CRIED' (2000)
Set in Europe between world wars, Cesar (Depp) is the
seductive gypsy loved by Suzie (Christina Ricci, left). /
In diesem Film, der in Europa zwischen den Weltkriegen
angesiedelt ist, spielt Depp den verführerischen
Zigeuner Cesar, den Suzie (Christina Ricci, links) liebt. /
Situé en Europe dans l'entre-deux-guerres, ce film
raconte l'histoire de Suzie (Christina Ricci, à gauche),
qui tombe amoureuse de César (Depp), un
séduisant tzigane.

STILL FROM 'THE MAN WHO CRIED' (2000)
The affair between Ricci's Jewish refugee and Depp's
gypsy is at the heart of Sally Potter's romance. / Die
Romanze zwischen dem jüdischen Flüchtling (Ricci)
und dem Zigeuner (Depp) steht im Mittelpunkt dieses
Liebesfilms von Sally Potter. / L'amour qui unit la jeune
réfugiée juive (Ricci) et le tzigane (Depp) est au cœur du
film de Sally Potter.

STILL FROM 'BEFORE NIGHT FALLS' (2000)
Depp plays two roles in this intimate epic, based on the memoirs of Cuban poet Reinaldo Arenas. Here he is Lieutenant Victor, a Cuban jailer. / Depp spielt in diesem intimen Epos nach dem autobiografischen Roman des kubanischen Dichters Reinaldo Arenas, *Bevor es Nacht wird*, zwei Rollen. Hier stellt er den kubanischen Gefängniswärter Teniente Victor dar. / Dans cette épopée intime tirée des mémoires du poète cubain Reinaldo Arenas, Depp interprète deux rôles, celui du lieutenant Victor, un geôlier cubain...

"If you turn on the television and see the horrors that are happening to people in the world right now, I think there's no better time to strive to have some kind of hope through imagination. I think it's a time to close your eyes and try to make a change, or at least hope to make a change, or we're going to explode."
Johnny Depp

„Wenn man den Fernseher anschaltet und die schrecklichen Dinge sieht, die Menschen heutzutage in der Welt passieren, dann gibt es, glaube ich, keinen besseren Zeitpunkt, um nach etwas Hoffnung durch Fantasie zu streben. Ich denke, es ist eine Zeit, in der man die Augen schließen und versuchen sollte, etwas zu verändern oder wenigstens zu hoffen, etwas zu verändern, sonst explodieren wir noch."
Johnny Depp

STILL FROM 'BEFORE NIGHT FALLS' (2000)
Here, as the angelic androgyne "Bon Bon," Depp is one of the jailed, opposite Javier Bardem as poet Reinaldo Arenas. / Und hier ist Depp als der engelhafte, androgyne „Bon Bon", einer der Häftlinge, neben Javier Bardem in der Rolle des Dichters Reinaldo Arenas zu sehen. / ... et celui de l'angélique travesti « Bon Bon », l'un des codétenus de Reinaldo Arenas (Javier Bardem).

PAGES 110/111
STILL FROM 'CHOCOLAT' (2000)
"One night I'll come by and take that squeak out of your door," Roux (Depp) tells chocolatier Vianne Rocher (Juliette Binoche). / „Eines Nachts komme ich vorbei und beseitige das Quietschen Ihrer Tür", verspricht Roux (Depp) der Chocolatière Vianne Rocher (Juliette Binoche). / « Un soir, je passerai m'occuper du grincement de votre porte », promet Roux (Depp) à la chocolatière Vianne Rocher (Juliette Binoche).

« Si vous allumez la télévision et que vous voyez les horreurs qui se passent dans le monde actuellement, je crois qu'il n'y a pas de meilleur moment pour tenter de faire naître une lueur d'espoir par le biais de l'imagination. C'est le moment de fermer les yeux et de tenter de changer les choses, ou du moins d'espérer les changer ; sinon, on va exploser. »
Johnny Depp

"You use your money to buy privacy because during most of your life you aren't allowed to be normal."
Johnny Depp

„Du benutzt dein Geld, um dir Privatsphäre zu erkaufen, weil dir während des größten Teils deines Lebens nicht gestattet wird, normal zu sein."
Johnny Depp

« Notre argent nous sert à acheter un peu d'intimité, car pendant la majeure partie de notre vie, on ne nous laisse pas être normal. »
Johnny Depp

STILL FROM 'BLOW' (2001)
George Jung (Depp) has the skill to succeed at anything, but he is desperate to become rich fast, and so turns to the drug trade. / George Jung (Depp) besitzt das Talent, überall erfolgreich zu sein, aber er will unbedingt schnell zu Geld kommen und steigt daher ins Drogengeschäft ein. / Bien qu'il soit doué pour tout, George Jung (Depp) succombe à la tentation de l'argent facile et se lance dans le trafic de drogue.

STILL FROM 'BLOW' (2001)
Jung's closest ally, Diego Delgado (Jordi Mollà),
becomes his most vicious adversary in a money-mad
world where loyalties are bought and sold. / Jungs
engster Verbündeter, Diego Delgado (Jordi Mollà), wird
zu seinem ärgsten Feind in einer vom Mammon
besessenen Welt, in der Loyalitäten gekauft und
verkauft werden. / Le principal allié de Jung, Diego
Delgado (Jordi Mollà), devient son adversaire le plus
acharné dans un monde régi par l'argent où la loyauté
s'achète et se vend.

STILL FROM 'BLOW' (2001)
George marries Mirtha (Penélope Cruz), the girl of
his dreams, but she is attracted to his wealth, which is
tragically fragile. / George heiratet Mirtha (Penélope
Cruz), die Frau seiner Träume, doch sie lockt nur sein
Reichtum, der sich tragischerweise als flüchtig erweist. /
Si George épouse Mirtha (Penélope Cruz), la fille de ses
rêves, celle-ci est surtout attirée par sa richesse, qui
s'avère terriblement fragile.

STILL FROM 'FROM HELL' (2001)

As Inspector Abberline, Depp must protect Mary Kelly (Heather Graham) as he tracks the killer into society's most powerful circles. / Als Inspector Abberline muss Depp Mary Kelly (Heather Graham) beschützen, während er den Mörder bis in die mächtigsten Kreise der Gesellschaft verfolgt. / Tandis que son enquête le mène vers les hautes sphères de la société, l'inspecteur Abberline (Depp) tente de protéger la jeune Mary Kelly (Heather Graham).

STILL FROM 'FROM HELL' (2001)

The hunt for the fabled killer Jack the Ripper drives this Hughes Brothers film, based on the graphic novel by Alan Moore and Eddie Campbell. / Die Jagd nach dem sagenumwobenen Serienmörder Jack the Ripper steht im Mittelpunkt dieses Films der Hughes-Brüder nach dem Comicroman von Alan Moore und Eddie Campbell. / Tiré d'un roman graphique d'Alan Moore et Eddie Campbell, le film des frères Hughes raconte la traque du célèbre Jack l'éventreur.

ON THE SET OF 'LOST IN LA MANCHA' (2002)
Here is a wonderful film that might have been—'Don Quixote' directed by Terry Gilliam, with Depp in the Sancho Panza role. / Es hätte ein wundervoller Film werden können: *Don Quijote* unter der Regie von Terry Gilliam und mit Depp als Sancho Panza. / Un film merveilleux aurait pu voir le jour : l'histoire de Don Quichotte réalisée par Terry Gilliam, avec Johnny Depp dans le rôle de Sancho Panza.

PAGES 118/119
STILL FROM 'FROM HELL' (2001)
A flawed hero, Abberline must also combat a weakness for opium, which seems to amplify his psychic abilities. / Abberline, ein Held mit Ecken und Kanten, hat auch mit seiner Schwäche für Opium zu kämpfen, das seine übersinnlichen Fähigkeiten zu steigern scheint. / Héros imparfait, Abberline doit également lutter contre son penchant pour l'opium, qui semble affûter ses capacités psychiques.

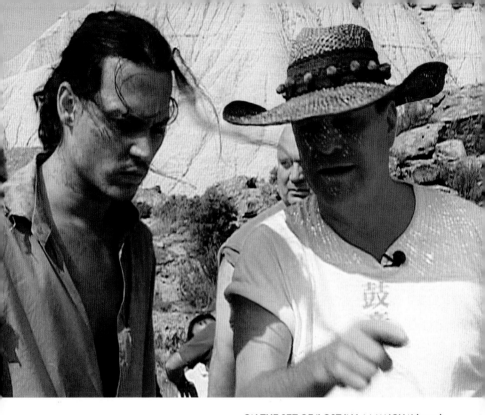

ON THE SET OF 'LOST IN LA MANCHA' (2002)
The film collapsed. What remains is this behind-the-scenes documentary directed by Keith Fulton and Louis Pepe. / Der Film kam nie zustande. Geblieben ist dieser Dokumentarfilm von Keith Fulton und Louis Pepe, der hinter die Kulissen des gescheiterten Projekts blickt. / Après l'abandon du projet, il ne reste qu'un documentaire retraçant le tournage, réalisé par Keith Fulton et Louis Pepe.

PAGES 122/123
STILL FROM 'LOST IN LA MANCHA' (2002)
Depp was to play a contemporary businessman, magically transported into the world of Don Quixote. / Depp sollte einen modernen Geschäftsmann spielen, der auf zauberhafte Weise in die Welt von Don Quijote transportiert wird. / Depp devait incarner un homme d'affaires contemporain, transporté par magie dans l'univers de Don Quichotte.

"Captain Jack Sparrow is like a cross between
Keith Richards and Pepé Le Pew."
Johnny Depp

„Käpt'n Jack Sparrow ist wie eine Kreuzung
zwischen Keith Richards und Pepé Le Pew [Pepe,
das Stinktier]."
Johnny Depp

« Le capitaine Jack Sparrow est une sorte de
croisement entre Keith Richards et Pépé le putois. »
Johnny Depp

**STILL FROM 'PIRATES OF THE CARIBBEAN:
THE CURSE OF THE BLACK PEARL' (2003)**
Depp's greatest box-office success to date has come in
the role of Captain Jack Sparrow, an ambitious but
comically off-kilter pirate. / Depps größter Kassenerfolg
ist bis heute die Rolle des Käpt'n Jack Sparrow, eines
ehrgeizigen, aber auf komische Weise durchgeknallten
Seeräubers. / Le plus grand succès de Johnny Depp au
box-office est à ce jour le rôle du capitaine Jack
Sparrow, pirate ambitieux mais délicieusement déjanté.

**STILL FROM 'PIRATES OF THE CARIBBEAN:
THE CURSE OF THE BLACK PEARL' (2003)**
Jack parries and trades quips with his rival in romance,
the gallant young swordsmith Will Turner (Orlando
Bloom). / Jack pariert und tauscht flotte Sprüche aus
mit seinem Rivalen in Herzensangelegenheiten, dem
galanten jungen Schwertschmied Will Turner (Orlando
Bloom). / Jack croise le fer et échange des mots d'esprit
avec son rival, le jeune et galant forgeron Will Turner
(Orlando Bloom).

*"I only wanted to be in a movie that my kids could
see."*
Johnny Depp on *Pirates of the Caribbean*

*„Ich wollte nur in einem Film mitspielen, den meine
Kinder sehen konnten."*
Johnny Depp über *Fluch der Karibik*

*« Je voulais seulement jouer dans un film que mes
enfants pourraient voir. »*
Johnny Depp à propos de *Pirates des Caraïbes*

**STILL FROM 'PIRATES OF THE CARIBBEAN:
THE CURSE OF THE BLACK PEARL' (2003)**
Although he is clever and relentless about regaining
command of his ship, Jack loses it again, and again. /
Obwohl er mit List und Hartnäckigkeit unablässig
versucht, das Kommando über sein Schiff
zurückzugewinnen, entgleitet es Jack immer wieder. /
Malgré son intelligence et sa détermination à
reconquérir son navire, Jack ne cesse de se le
faire dérober.

STILL FROM 'PIRATES OF THE CARIBBEAN: THE CURSE OF THE BLACK PEARL' (2003)
Jack Sparrow's trademark is a winning smile that promises endless mischief throughout this popular series. / Jack Sparrows Markenzeichen ist sein verschmitztes Lächeln, das während der gesamten beliebten Filmreihe nie enden wollende Turbulenzen verheißt. / La marque de fabrique de Jack Sparrow est un sourire enjôleur, annonciateur d'espiègleries en cascade tout au long de la série.

"Awards are not as important to me as when I meet a 10-year-old kid who says, 'I love Captain Jack Sparrow'—that's real magic for me."
Johnny Depp

„Auszeichnungen sind mir nicht so wichtig, wie wenn ich einen Zehnjährigen treffe, der sagt: ‚Ich liebe Käpt'n Jack Sparrow!' – das ist für mich echter Zauber."
Johnny Depp

« Recevoir un prix n'est pas aussi important à mes yeux que de rencontrer un gamin de 10 ans qui me dit : "J'adore le capitaine Jack Sparrow." Ça, c'est vraiment magique. »
Johnny Depp

STILL FROM 'ONCE UPON A TIME IN MEXICO' (2003)
His stolen kiss with Ajedrez (Eva Mendes) is directly on target. / Der letzte Kuss mit Ajedrez (Eva Mendes) trifft genau das Ziel. / Son baiser volé à Ajedrez (Eva Mendes) est en plein dans le mille.

STILL FROM 'ONCE UPON A TIME IN MEXICO' (2003)
Even without his eyes, the renegade CIA assassin Sands (Depp) is still the fastest draw and the surest shot south of the border. / Selbst ohne sein Augenlicht ist der abtrünnige CIA-Killer Sands (Depp) noch immer der schnellste und treffsicherste Schütze südlich der Grenze. / Même privé de ses yeux, Sands (Depp), agent corrompu de la CIA, demeure la gâchette la plus rapide et la plus précise du Mexique.

"As a teenager I was so insecure. I was the type of guy that never fit in because he never dared to choose. I was convinced I had absolutely no talent at all. For nothing. And that thought took away all my ambition, too."
Johnny Depp

„Als Teenager war ich so unsicher. Ich war der Typ von Kerl, der in keine Gruppe passte, weil ich mich nie entscheiden konnte. Ich war davon überzeugt, dass ich absolut überhaupt kein Talent besaß – zu gar nichts. Und das nahm mir auch meinen ganzen Ehrgeiz."
Johnny Depp

« À l'adolescence, je n'avais aucune confiance en moi. J'étais le genre de mec qui ne s'intègre jamais car il n'arrive pas à se décider. J'étais persuadé de n'avoir absolument aucun talent pour rien. Et du coup, je n'avais aucune ambition. »
Johnny Depp

ON THE SET OF 'ONCE UPON A TIME IN MEXICO' (2003)
Rehearsing a move with director Robert Rodriguez. / Depp probt eine Bewegung mit Regisseur Robert Rodriguez. / Répétition d'un mouvement avec le metteur en scène Robert Rodriguez.

STILL FROM 'SECRET WINDOW' (2004)
Mort Rainey (Depp) is a divorced writer still hoping to
get together with his wife in this adaptation of a Stephen
King story. / Mort Rainey (Depp) ist ein geschiedener
Schriftsteller, der in dieser Verfilmung einer Erzählung
von Stephen King hofft, dass seine Frau doch noch zu
ihm zurückfindet. / Adapté d'une nouvelle de Stephen
King, ce film est l'histoire de Mort Rainey (Depp), un
écrivain divorcé qui espère se réconcilier avec sa
femme.

"I can remember when I finished Edward
Scissorhands, *looking in the mirror as the girl was
doing my makeup for the last time and thinking—it
was like the 90th or 89th day of shooting—and I
remember looking and going, 'Wow, this is it. I'm
saying goodbye to this guy, I'm saying goodbye to
Edward Scissorhands.' You know, it was kind of sad.
But in fact, I think they're all still somehow in there."*
Johnny Depp

*„Ich kann mich erinnern, wie ich dachte, als ich
Edward mit den Scherenhänden abschloss und
in den Spiegel sah, während das Mädchen zum
letzten Mal meine Maske machte - es war der 90.
oder 89. Drehtag: ‚Wow! Das war's! Ich verabschiede
mich von diesem Kerl. Ich sage Tschüss zu Edward.'
Wissen Sie, es war irgendwie traurig. Aber in
Wirklichkeit, glaube ich, stecken sie alle noch
irgendwie in mir drin."*
Johnny Depp

STILL FROM 'SECRET WINDOW' (2004)
A mysterious stranger, John Shooter (John Turturro), violently accuses Mort Rainey of stealing his ideas. / Der geheimnisvolle Fremde John Shooter (John Turturro) beschuldigt Mort Rainey unter Anwendung von Gewalt, seine Ideen gestohlen zu haben. / Un mystérieux inconnu, John Shooter (John Turturro), accuse Mort Rainey de plagiat.

« Quand j'ai fini Edward aux mains d'argent, je me rappelle que je me suis regardé dans le miroir pendant que la fille faisait mon maquillage pour la dernière fois – ce devait être le 90ᵉ ou 89ᵉ jour de tournage – et que je me suis dit : "Voilà, c'est fini. Je quitte ce gars, je dis au revoir à Edward." C'était assez triste. Mais en réalité, je crois qu'ils sont tous encore en moi. »
Johnny Depp

STILL FROM 'FINDING NEVERLAND' (2004)
J. M. Barrie, the creator of Peter Pan, is shy with adults
but plays freely with children—being a child at heart
himself. / J. M. Barrie, der Schöpfer des Peter Pan, ist
schüchtern im Umgang mit Erwachsenen, aber fröhlich
und frei im Kreise von Kindern, weil er selbst im Herzen
ein Kind geblieben ist. / Demeuré un enfant dans l'âme,
J. M. Barrie, le créateur de Peter Pan, se montre timide
avec les adultes mais très à l'aise avec les enfants.

*"With any part you play, there is a certain amount
of yourself in it. There has to be, otherwise it's just
not acting. It's lying."*
Johnny Depp

„*In jeder Rolle, die du spielst, steckt ein bestimmter
Anteil von dir selbst drin. Das muss so sein, sonst
ist es einfach keine Schauspielerei. Dann ist es
Lügen.*"
Johnny Depp

« *Quel que soit le rôle que vous jouez, vous y
mettez un peu de vous. Forcément, sinon ce ne
serait pas un travail d'acteur. Ce serait un
mensonge.* »
Johnny Depp

STILL FROM 'FINDING NEVERLAND' (2004)
Barrie was a prolific, and not always financially
successful playwright, so he was dependent on the
good graces of his producer Charles Frohman (Dustin
Hoffman). / Barrie war einst ein Dramatiker, der zwar
viel schrieb, aber finanziell nicht immer erfolgreich und
somit vom guten Willen seines Intendanten Charles
Frohman (Dustin Hoffman) abhängig war. / Dramaturge
prolifique mais pas toujours prospère, Barrie dépend
des bonnes grâces de son producteur, Charles Frohman
(Dustin Hoffman).

PAGES 138/139
STILL FROM 'FINDING NEVERLAND' (2004)
Barrie is in love with Sylvia Llewelyn Davies (Kate
Winslet) and her brood of energetic boys (among them
Freddie Highmore, right). / Barrie liebt Sylvia Llewelyn
Davies (Kate Winslet) und ihre Brut wilder Burschen
(darunter Freddie Highmore, rechts). / Barrie s'éprend
de Sylvia Llewelyn Davies (Kate Winslet) et de sa flopée
de garçons remuants (parmi lesquels Freddie Highmore,
à droite).

STILL FROM 'THE LIBERTINE' (2004)
As poet John Wilmot, Earl of Rochester, who fiercely
refused to pay routine homage to his king, Charles II. /
Als Dichter John Wilmot, Graf von Rochester, der sich
vehement weigerte, seinem König, Charles II., die
übliche Ehrerbietung zu erweisen. / Dans le rôle du
poète John Wilmot, comte de Rochester, qui refuse
farouchement de rendre l'hommage de rigueur à son
roi, Charles II.

STILL FROM 'THE LIBERTINE' (2004)
Rochester's contrarian spirit struck a chord deep in
that corner of Depp's heart where Marlon Brando and
Hunter S. Thompson still flourish. / Rochesters
aufsässige Einstellung traf einen Nerv tief im Herzen
von Johnny Depp, wo Marlon Brando und Hunter S.
Thompson weiterleben. / L'esprit anticonformiste de
Rochester touche une corde sensible au fond du cœur
de Depp, là où demeure vivace la mémoire de Marlon
Brando et de Hunter S. Thompson.

STILL FROM 'THE LIBERTINE' (2004)
Conspicuously irritating his devoted wife, Elizabeth
(Rosamund Pike), by posing her with a monkey (just out
of frame, at left). / Seine hingebungsvolle Ehefrau
Elizabeth (Rosamund Pike) verwirrt er sichtlich, indem
er sie mit einem Affen (links außerhalb des
Bildausschnitts) posieren lässt. / Rochester irrite
délibérément Elizabeth (Rosamund Pike), son épouse
dévouée, en la faisant poser avec un singe (hors cadre
sur la gauche).

*"The only thing that matters in life is being a good
parent. I can't say the darkness is completely gone.
It's still there—but I've never been closer to the light
than I am these days."*
Johnny Depp

„*Das Einzige, worauf es im Leben ankommt, ist,
gute Eltern zu sein. Ich kann nicht sagen, dass die
Finsternis vollkommen verschwunden ist. Sie ist
noch da - aber ich war dem Licht noch nie näher
als heute.*"
Johnny Depp

« *La seule chose qui compte dans la vie, c'est d'être
un bon parent. Je ne peux pas dire que les
ténèbres aient totalement disparu. Elles sont
toujours là. Mais je n'ai jamais été aussi proche de
la lumière qu'aujourd'hui.* »
Johnny Depp

STILL FROM 'THE LIBERTINE' (2004)
His verbal genius and moral passion might have made
him a great to set beside Shakespeare, but he rebelled,
even against himself. / Mit seinem verbalen Genie und
seiner moralischen Passion hätte er einen Platz neben
Shakespeare unter den ganz Großen seiner Zeit finden
können, doch er rebellierte – sogar gegen sich selbst. /
Son génie verbal et sa passion morale auraient pu faire
de lui un écrivain de la trempe de Shakespeare, mais il
se rebelle également contre lui-même.

STILL FROM 'CHARLIE AND THE CHOCOLATE FACTORY' (2005)
Roald Dahl's enigmatic candy maker, Willy Wonka, presented a ripe opportunity for lively collaboration between Depp and director Tim Burton. / Roald Dahls undurchschaubarer Süßwarenfabrikant Willy Wonka bot eine perfekte Gelegenheit für ein weiteres quirlig-spritziges Gemeinschaftswerk von Depp und Regisseur Tim Burton. / Willy Wonka, l'énigmatique confiseur du roman de Roald Dahl, offre à Johnny Depp et au cinéaste Tim Burton l'occasion d'une nouvelle collaboration endiablée.

"The only creatures that are evolved enough to convey pure love are dogs and infants."
Johnny Depp

„Die einzigen Geschöpfe, die weit genug entwickelt sind, um reine Liebe auszudrücken, sind Hunde und Kleinkinder."
Johnny Depp

« Les seules créatures assez évoluées pour exprimer un amour pur sont les chiens et les jeunes enfants. »
Johnny Depp

STILL FROM 'CHARLIE AND THE CHOCOLATE FACTORY' (2005)
Welcome to Depp-Burton Land, ideally sweet and insidiously dark. / Willkommen im Depp-Burton-Land, perfekt gesüßt und doch tückisch düster. / Bienvenue au pays de Depp-Burton, idéalement sucré et insidieusement inquiétant.

PAGES 146/147
STILL FROM 'CHARLIE AND THE CHOCOLATE FACTORY' (2005)
Depp based his performance on legendary billionaire Howard Hughes and "various rock stars." Pop icon Michael Jackson comes to mind. / Depp gründete seine Interpretation der Rolle auf dem legendären Milliardär Howard Hughes und „diversen Rockstars" – spontan kommt Popikone Michael Jackson in den Sinn. / Pour ce rôle, Depp s'inspire du célèbre milliardaire Howard Hughes et de « diverses rock stars » ; on pense évidemment à Michael Jackson.

148

"There's nothing else like music. Nothing that touches us on that deep level. Music can open up so many emotions that we didn't know we had. That's the magical thing about musicals, on the stage or on film. Love songs. They work so well because the music touches us, emotionally, where words alone can't."
Johnny Depp

„Es gibt nichts, das wie Musik ist – nichts, was uns ähnlich tief berührt. Musik kann so viele Gefühle wecken, von denen wir nie wussten, dass es sie gibt. Das ist das Zauberhafte an Musicals, ob auf der Bühne oder im Film. Liebeslieder: Sie funktionieren so gut, weil uns die Musik emotional berührt, wo Worte allein versagen."
Johnny Depp

« Rien ne vaut la musique. Rien ne nous touche aussi profondément. La musique éveille tant d'émotions dont on ne soupçonne même pas l'existence. C'est ce qui fait la magie des comédies musicales, sur scène comme au cinéma. Les chansons d'amour : si elles marchent si bien, c'est parce que la musique nous touche émotionnellement là où les mots ne suffiraient pas. »
Johnny Depp

STILL FROM 'CHARLIE AND THE CHOCOLATE FACTORY' (2005)
The madcap gadgetry here is well up to the Tim Burton standard. / Die verrückten technischen Spielereien hier entsprechen der üblichen Ausstattung eines Tim-Burton-Films. / Les gadgets délirants de la chocolaterie sont conformes à l'esprit de Tim Burton.

STILL FROM 'CHARLIE AND THE CHOCOLATE FACTORY' (2005)
An annoying child, much reduced in size. The protective goggles are pure Elton John. / Ein nerviges Kind wird buchstäblich zurechtgestutzt. Die Schutzbrille ist eine eindeutige Hommage an Elton John. / Un enfant agaçant devenu lilliputien sous le regard médusé d'adultes munis de lunettes dignes d'Elton John.

"I think it's an actor's responsibility to change every time. Not only for himself and the people he's working with, but for the audience. If you just go out and deliver the same dish every time ... it's meat loaf again ... you'd get bored. I'd get bored."
Johnny Depp

„Ich denke, ein Schauspieler trägt die Verantwortung, sich jedes Mal zu verändern. Nicht nur für sich selbst und die Leute, mit denen er arbeitet, sondern für das Publikum. Wenn du nur rausgehst und jedes Mal das gleiche Gericht auftischst – ‚schon wieder Hackbraten!' –, dann wird es langweilig. Ich würde mich langweilen."
Johnny Depp

**STILL FROM 'CHARLIE AND THE
CHOCOLATE FACTORY' (2005)**
Notice the lively detail with which Tim Burton visualizes
his characters, from head to toe. / Man beachte die
witzigen Details, mit denen Tim Burton seine Figuren
von Kopf bis Fuß ausstattet. / Notez les détails piquants
dont Tim Burton affuble ses personnages des pieds à
la tête.

PAGES 152/153
STILL FROM 'CORPSE BRIDE' (2005)
In this animated fantasy produced by Tim Burton,
the bridegroom Victor Van Dort (voiced by Depp) is
designed to look like Depp, too. / In diesem von Tim
Burton produzierten Animationsfilm spricht Bräutigam
Victor Van Dort (im Original) nicht nur mit der Stimme
von Depp, sondern sieht auch so aus. / Dans ce conte
d'animation réalisé par Tim Burton, le jeune époux,
Victor Van Dort, possède la voix et l'apparence de
Johnny Depp.

« Un acteur se doit de changer à chaque fois. Non
seulement pour lui-même et pour les gens avec qui
il travaille, mais aussi pour le public. Si vous vous
contentez de resservir tout le temps le même plat
– "encore un steak !" –, on finit par s'ennuyer. Moi,
en tout cas, je finirais par m'ennuyer. »
Johnny Depp

"I'm an old-fashioned guy ... I want to be an old man with a beer belly sitting on a porch, looking at a lake or something."
Johnny Depp

„Ich bin ein altmodischer Typ ... Ich möchte ein alter Mann werden mit einem Bierbauch, der auf einer Veranda sitzt und auf einen See hinausschaut oder so was."
Johnny Depp

« Je suis assez vieux jeu [...]. Quand je serai vieux, je veux avoir de la brioche et m'asseoir sur une terrasse en admirant un lac ou je ne sais quoi. »
Johnny Depp

STILL FROM 'PIRATES OF THE CARIBBEAN: DEAD MAN'S CHEST' (2006)
The huge success of the first 'Pirates' film dictated that there be a second, and third. / Auf den Riesenerfolg des ersten *Fluch der Karibik* folgten zwangsläufig ein zweiter und ein dritter. / L'immense succès du premier *Pirates des Caraïbes* entraîne le tournage d'un deuxième puis d'un troisième film.

**ON THE SET OF 'PIRATES OF THE
CARIBBEAN: DEAD MAN'S CHEST' (2006)**
Depp takes his cue from director Gore Verbinski
(center). / Depp erhält Anweisungen von Regisseur
Gore Verbinski (Mitte). / Depp suit les instructions du
réalisateur, Gore Verbinski (au centre).

*"I'm shy, paranoid, whatever word you want to use.
I hate fame. I've done everything I can to avoid it."*
Johnny Depp

*„Ich bin schüchtern, paranoid – welchen Begriff Sie
auch benutzen möchten. Ich hasse Ruhm. Ich habe
alles getan, was ich konnte, um ihn zu vermeiden."*
Johnny Depp

*« Je suis timide ou parano, appelez ça comme vous
voulez. Je déteste la célébrité. J'ai tout fait pour
l'éviter. »*
Johnny Depp

STILL FROM 'PIRATES OF THE CARIBBEAN: DEAD MAN'S CHEST' (2006)
Jack Sparrow gets to heap fresh torments on his virtuous rival, Will Turner (Orlando Bloom). / Jack Sparrow denkt sich neue Qualen für seinen tugendhaften Rivalen Will Turner (Orlando Bloom) aus. / Jack Sparrow fait subir une nouvelle avalanche de supplices à son vertueux rival, Will Turner (Orlando Bloom).

"I've been around long enough to know that one week, you're on the exclusive list of guys who can open a movie, and then the next week, you're off the list. It's been a fun ride, and I'm enjoying it for all it's worth."
Johnny Depp

„Ich bin lange genug im Geschäft, um zu wissen, dass du in der einen Woche auf der exklusiven Liste der Typen stehen kannst, die einen Film tragen können, und in der nächsten Woche bist du von der Liste verschwunden. Der Ausflug hat Spaß gemacht, und ich genieße es, solange es geht."
Johnny Depp

« Je suis depuis assez longtemps dans le métier pour savoir qu'un jour, on appartient au club très fermé des gens qui font vendre les films, et le lendemain, on est rayé de la liste. C'est une expérience amusante et j'en profite, pour ce que ça vaut. »
Johnny Depp

STILL FROM 'PIRATES OF THE CARIBBEAN: DEAD MAN'S CHEST' (2006)
This middle panel in the trilogy is—deliberately—the darkest and least crowd-pleasing, the better to propel the climaxes of Part Three. / Diese mittlere Episode der Trilogie ist - absichtlich - die düsterste und die am wenigsten publikumsträchtige, damit die Höhepunkte in Teil 3 noch besser zum Ausdruck kommen. / Le deuxième volet de la trilogie est volontairement le plus sombre et le moins accrocheur pour le grand public, afin de mieux mettre en valeur les temps forts de la troisième partie.

STILL FROM 'PIRATES OF THE CARIBBEAN: DEAD MAN'S CHEST' (2006)
Battling Norrington (Jack Davenport) and Will Turner for the heart of Davy Jones. / Mit Norrington (Jack Davenport) und Will Turner kämpft er gleichzeitig um das Herz von Davy Jones. / En plein combat avec Norrington (Jack Davenport) et Will Turner pour récupérer le cœur de Davy Jones.

PAGES 162/163
STILL FROM 'PIRATES OF THE CARIBBEAN: DEAD MAN'S CHEST' (2006)
In close conference with the ghostly ghoul, Bootstrap Bill (Stellan Skarsgård). / Jack berät sich mit dem garstigen Gespenst Bootstrap Bill (Stellan Skarsgård). / En tête-à-tête avec une repoussante créature nommée Bill le Bottier (Stellan Skarsgård).

STILL FROM 'PIRATES OF THE CARIBBEAN: DEAD MAN'S CHEST' (2006)
As usual, at odds with the governor's lovely daughter, Elizabeth Swann (Keira Knightley). / Wie üblich hat Jack Probleme mit Elizabeth Swann (Keira Knightley), der liebreizenden Tochter des Gouverneurs. / Comme toujours en désaccord avec Elizabeth Swann (Keira Knightley), la ravissante fille du gouverneur.

STILL FROM 'PIRATES OF THE CARIBBEAN: AT WORLD'S END' (2007)
Captain Jack plans to impress two ladies (Vanessa Branch and Lauren Maher), not knowing his boat has once again been taken. / Käpt'n Jack möchte zwei Damen (Vanessa Branch und Lauren Maher) beeindrucken und weiß noch nicht, dass sein Schiff schon wieder entführt wurde. / Désireux d'impressionner deux demoiselles (Vanessa Branch et Lauren Maher), le capitaine Jack ignore que son navire a de nouveau été dérobé.

"Most of what's been written about me has been completely false. People have created an image that has absolutely nothing to do with me, and they have the power to sell it, to shove it down the throats of people. I'm an old-fashioned guy who wants marriage and kids."
Johnny Depp

„Das meiste, was über mich geschrieben wurde, war vollkommen falsch. Die Leute haben ein Image geschaffen, das absolut nichts mit mir zu tun hat, und sie besitzen die Macht, es zu verkaufen, es den Menschen in den Rachen zu schieben. Ich bin ein altmodischer Kerl, der heiraten und Kinder haben will."
Johnny Depp

**STILL FROM 'PIRATES OF THE CARIBBEAN:
AT WORLD'S END' (2007)**
Caught in the clutches of Captain Sao Feng (Chow
Yun-Fat). One great pleasure of these three films is
their wealth of colorful roles and performances. / In
den Fängen von Käpt'n Sao Feng (Chow Yun-Fat): Ein
großes Vergnügen bereitet in diesen drei Filmen die
Fülle an farbenfrohen Rollen und schillernden
schauspielerischen Leistungen. / Entre les griffes du
capitaine Sao Feng (Chow Yun-Fat). L'un des attraits de
cette trilogie est sa brochette de personnages hauts en
couleur interprétés avec truculence.

*« La plupart des choses qui ont été écrites à mon
sujet sont totalement fausses. Certains ont créé
une image qui n'a absolument rien à voir avec moi
et ont été en mesure de la vendre et de la faire
gober au public. Je suis un mec vieux jeu qui veut
se marier et faire des enfants. »*
Johnny Depp

PAGES 166/167
**ON THE SET OF 'PIRATES OF THE
CARIBBEAN: AT WORLD'S END' (2007)**
A crew of craftspeople to match the crew comprising
(left to right) Geoffrey Rush, Keira Knightley, and
Depp. / Ein Tross an Mitarbeitern für die Piraten-
mannschaft aus (von links nach rechts) Geoffrey Rush,
Keira Knightley und Depp. / Toute une équipe de
techniciens s'affaire autour de l'équipage composé
(de gauche à droite) de Geoffrey Rush, Keira Knightley
et Johnny Depp.

**STILL FROM 'PIRATES OF THE CARIBBEAN:
AT WORLD'S END' (2007)**
Depp famously modeled Captain Jack on Rolling Stones
guitarist Keith Richards, and Richards repaid the
compliment with a cameo as Jack's father. / Es ist wohl-
bekannt, dass Depp seinen Käpt'n Jack dem Gitarristen
der Rolling Stones, Keith Richards, nachempfand, der
das Kompliment durch einen Cameo-Auftritt als Jacks
Vater erwiderte. / Depp ayant déclaré qu'il s'était
inspiré de Keith Richards pour le personnage de Jack
Sparrow, le guitariste des Rolling Stones lui rend la
politesse en apparaissant brièvement dans le rôle du
père de Jack.

**PORTRAIT FOR 'PIRATES OF THE
CARIBBEAN: AT WORLD'S END' (2007)**
Here is the role for which at least one generation of
children will forever remember Johnny Depp. / Hier ist
die Rolle, für die mindestens eine Generation von
Kindern Johnny Depp ewig in Erinnerung behalten
wird. / Le rôle dans lequel au moins une génération
d'enfants se souviendra de Johnny Depp.

**STILL FROM 'SWEENEY TODD: THE DEMON
BARBER OF FLEET STREET' (2007)**
A vengeful onlooker, brandishing his lethal razor amid
a throng of otherwise preoccupied passersby. / Ein
rachsüchtiger Zaungast, der sein tödliches Rasier-
messer inmitten anderweitig beschäftigter Passanten
schwingt. / Le barbier vengeur brandissant son
redoutable rasoir au milieu d'une foule de passants
indifférents.

PAGES 170/171
**STILL FROM 'SWEENEY TODD: THE DEMON
BARBER OF FLEET STREET' (2007)**
Sweeney Todd, Depp's darkest role and his most
demanding—required him to kill ruthlessly, sing
beautifully, yet be sympathetic. / Sweeney Todd, Depps
düsterste und anspruchsvollste Rolle, verlangte von ihm,
dass er rücksichtslos mordete, wunderschön sang und
trotzdem sympathisch wirkte. / Sweeney Todd est le
rôle le plus sombre et le plus exigeant de sa carrière,
puisqu'il doit incarner un tueur impitoyable doublé d'un
chanteur agréable sans perdre la sympathie du public.

STILL FROM 'SWEENEY TODD: THE DEMON BARBER OF FLEET STREET' (2007)
He is singing to us of his deadly intentions, of which the world (among them this pedestrian) remains blissfully ignorant. / Dem Zuschauer erzählt er singend von seinen tödlichen Absichten, von denen die Welt (darunter auch dieser Passant) völlig ahnungslos bleibt. / Sweeney Todd nous confie en chansons ses funestes intentions, que le reste du monde (et notamment ce passant) continue d'ignorer.

"[Tim Burton] can ask me everything. If he wants me to have sex with an aardvark in one of his next movies, then I will do that."
Johnny Depp

„[Tim Burton] kann alles von mir verlangen. Wenn er will, dass ich in einem seiner Filme Sex mit einem Erdferkel habe, dann mach ich das."
Johnny Depp

« [Tim Burton] peut me demander n'importe quoi. S'il veut que je me tape un phacochère dans un de ses prochains films, je le ferai. »
Johnny Depp

STILL FROM 'SWEENEY TODD: THE DEMON BARBER OF FLEET STREET' (2007)
Waltzing with Mrs. Lovett (Helena Bonham Carter), a terrible cook but a resourceful disposer of corpses. / Beim Walzer mit Mrs. Lovett (Helena Bonham Carter), die fürchterlich kocht, aber sehr gut Leichen verschwinden lassen kann. / Quelques pas de valse avec Mrs. Lovett (Helena Bonham Carter), piètre cuisinière mais très douée pour faire disparaître les corps.

PAGES 176/177
STILL FROM 'SWEENEY TODD: THE DEMON BARBER OF FLEET STREET' (2007)
The iconic Johnny Depp—ever sharp-edged, ever intense, ever lyrical (with Alan Rickman). / Johnny Depp, wie man ihn kennt: scharfkantig, konzentriert und gefühlvoll (mit Alan Rickman). / Johnny Depp comme on l'aime : incisif, lyrique et ténébreux (avec Alan Rickman).

STILL FROM 'SWEENEY TODD: THE DEMON BARBER OF FLEET STREET' (2007)
Working again with director Tim Burton, Depp provides the personal magnetic force around which Burton's nightmare world freely revolves. / Wieder einmal unter der Regie von Tim Burton liefert Depps Figur den Magnetpol, um den sich Burtons albtraumhafte Welt frei dreht. / De nouveau associé à Tim Burton, Depp constitue le pôle magnétique autour duquel gravite l'univers cauchemardesque du cinéaste.

3
CHRONOLOGY

CHRONOLOGIE

CHRONOLOGIE

CHRONOLOGY

9 June 1963 Born John Christopher Depp in Owensboro, Kentucky. Fourth child and second son of Betty Sue Wells Depp and John Depp Sr. His ancestry is profoundly American: of the Cherokee tribe on his mother's side and, on his father's, descended from Pierre Deppe—a French Huguenot who fled religious persecution by escaping to Virginia in 1697.

Circa 1969 At age six, a devoted fan of Buster Keaton and Lon Chaney, owing to a popular afternoon TV show, *Silents, Please.*

1970 Family moves to Miramar, Florida.

1971–1978 Learns to play guitar. Parents divorce. Depp stays close by his mother. Flunks out of high school; forms a rock band, The Kids.

1983 Leaves Florida; moves to Los Angeles. Works menial odd jobs—pumping gas, working construction, selling ballpoint pens by telephone. December 20: Marries aspiring musician Lori Anne Allison (divorced 1985).

1984 At the urging of friend Nicolas Cage, takes a meeting with Cage's agent, Ilene Feldman, who secures Depp an audition for Wes Craven's *A Nightmare on Elm Street*—his film debut.

1986 Supporting role in Oliver Stone's Oscar-winning *Platoon*.

1987–1990 Stars in the hit TV series *21 Jump Street.*

1990 Fearing that *21 Jump Street* had defined him as "plastered, postered, patented, painted plastic," jumps at chance to redefine his image, working with cult directors John Waters and Tim Burton on *Cry-Baby* and *Edward Scissorhands*, respectively. Defines his career along these iconoclastic, idiosyncratic lines.

1998 After varied romantic involvements, most famously with actress Winona Ryder (1989–1993)

and English model Kate Moss (1994–1997), Depp meets singer-actress Vanessa Paradis (*The Girl on the Bridge*, 1999). To date, Depp makes his primary home with Paradis in Europe.

27 May 1999 Birth of daughter Lily-Rose Melody.

2000 September–October: Joins Terry Gilliam in Spain to film *The Man Who Killed Don Quixote*, a project of ripe promise undone by a series of catastrophes.

9 April 2002 Birth of son Jack John Christopher.

2004 Deaths of two great friends and role models: Hunter S. Thompson and Marlon Brando.

2003–2007 Redefines his career playing Jack Sparrow in the Disney megafranchise *Pirates of the Caribbean*. Years of playing eccentrics, defying categories, pay off in his popular characterization of this quasi-effeminate, quasi-inebriated superpirate.

PORTRAIT FOR 'CRY-BABY' (1990)

PAGE 178
STILL FROM 'DON JUAN DEMARCO' (1995)

CHRONOLOGIE

9. Juni 1963 Er kommt als John Christopher Depp in Owensboro (Kentucky) als viertes Kind und zweiter Sohn von Betty Sue Wells Depp und John Depp sen. zur Welt. Seine Ahnentafel ist typisch amerikanisch: Mütterlicherseits stammt er von Cherokee-Indianern ab und väterlicherseits von Pierre Deppe, einem französischen Hugenotten, der 1697 auf der Flucht vor religiöser Verfolgung in Virginia landete.

um 1969 Im Alter von sechs Jahren wird er dank einer beliebten Nachmittagssendung im Fernsehen mit dem Titel *Silents, Please* zu einem großen Verehrer der Stummfilmstars Buster Keaton und Lon Chaney.

1970 Die Familie zieht nach Miramar (Florida) um.

1971–1978 Lernt Gitarre zu spielen. Die Eltern lassen sich scheiden. Depp bleibt in der Nähe seiner Mutter. Er fliegt von der Highschool und tritt der Rockband The Kids bei.

1983 Verlässt Florida und zieht nach Los Angeles um. Er nimmt verschiedene Jobs an – an Tankstellen, auf Baustellen, als Verkäufer von Kugelschreibern per Telefon. 20. Dezember: heiratet die aufstrebende Musikerin Lori Anne Allison (Scheidung 1985).

1984 Auf Drängen seines Freundes Nicolas Cage trifft er sich mit dessen Agentin Ilene Feldman, die Depp ein Vorsprechen für Wes Cravens Film *Nightmare – Mörderische Träume* organisiert – sein Filmdebüt.

1986 Nebenrolle in Oliver Stones „Oscar"-prämiertem Film *Platoon*.

1987–1990 Spielt eine der Hauptrollen in der erfolgreichen Fernsehserie *21 Jump Street*.

1990 Aus Furcht, *21 Jump Street* könne ihn zu einer „erstarrten, plakatierten, patentierten Plastikpuppe" abstempeln, packt er die Gelegenheit beim Schopf, sein Image neu auszurichten, indem er mit den Kultregisseuren John Waters und Tim Burton in *Cry-Baby* bzw. *Edward mit den Scherenhänden* zusammenarbeitet. Er richtet seine Karriere entlang dieser ikonoklastischen, idiosynkratischen Linien aus.

1998 Nach diversen Beziehungen – am berühmtesten waren jene zu der Schauspielerin Winona Ryder (1989–1993) und dem britischen Fotomodell Kate Moss (1994–1997) – trifft Depp die französische Sängerin und Schauspielerin Vanessa Paradis (*Die Frau auf der Brücke*, 1999). Bis heute haben Depp und Paradis ihren Hauptwohnsitz in Europa.

27. Mai 1999 Geburt der Tochter Lily-Rose Melody.

2000 September/Oktober: Er reist zu Terry Gilliam nach Spanien zu den Dreharbeiten für *The Man Who Killed Don Quixote*, ein vielversprechendes Projekt, das durch eine Reihe von Katastrophen vereitelt wird.

9. April 2002 Geburt des Sohns Jack John Christopher.

2004 Tod zweier großer Freunde und Vorbilder: Hunter S. Thompson und Marlon Brando.

2003–2007 Er richtet seine Karriere neu aus, indem er Jack Sparrow in dem Disney-Mega-Franchise *Pirates of the Caribbean* spielt. All die Jahre, in denen er Exzentriker spielte, die sich in keine Schublade stecken ließen, zahlen sich aus in der populären Charakterisierung dieses quasiweibischen, quasibetrunkenen Superpiraten.

PORTRAIT FOR '21 JUMP STREET' (1987–1990)

CHRONOLOGIE

9 juin 1963 John Christopher Depp, fils de Betty Sue Wells Depp et John Depp Sr., naît à Owensboro, dans le Kentucky. Il a deux sœurs et un frère aîné. D'origine typiquement américaine, il a du sang cherokee par sa mère et descend par son père de Pierre Deppe, un Huguenot arrivé en Virginie en 1697 pour fuir les persécutions religieuses.

vers 1969 À six ans, Johnny devient un fan inconditionnel de Buster Keaton et de Lon Chaney grâce à l'émission *Silents, Please* consacrée au cinéma muet.

1970 La famille déménage à Miramar, en Floride.

1971–1978 Apprend la guitare. Après le divorce de ses parents, Johnny reste proche de sa mère, quitte l'école et fonde un groupe de rock, The Kids.

1983 Quitte la Floride pour Los Angeles. Vit de petits boulots : pompiste, ouvrier du bâtiment, vendeur de stylos par téléphone. 20 décembre : épouse la maquilleuse Lori Anne Allison (divorce en 1985).

1984 Son ami Nicolas Cage insiste pour lui présenter son agent, Ilene Feldman, qui décroche une audition pour *Les Griffes de la nuit* de Wes Craven, son premier film.

1986 Rôle secondaire dans *Platoon* d'Oliver Stone, récompensé par 4 oscars.

1987–1990 Rôle principal dans la célèbre série télévisée *21 Jump Street*.

1990 Craignant que *21 Jump Street* l'enferme dans une image propre et aseptisée, il joue dans *Cry-Baby* de John Waters et *Edward aux mains d'argent* de Tim Burton, deux cinéastes cultes qui vont réorienter sa carrière vers des rôles plus iconoclastes et plus personnels.

1998 Après différentes liaisons, notamment avec l'actrice Winona Ryder (1989-1993) et le top model anglais Kate Moss (1994-1997), Depp rencontre la chanteuse et comédienne Vanessa Paradis (*La Fille sur le pont*, 1999), avec laquelle il possède une résidence principale en France.

27 mai 1999 Naissance de sa fille, Lily-Rose Melody.

2000 Septembre-octobre : rejoint Terry Gilliam en Espagne pour le tournage de *L'Homme qui tua Don Quichotte*, un projet prometteur anéanti par une séries de catastrophes.

9 avril 2002 Naissance de son fils, Jack John Christopher.

2004 Décès de deux grands amis et modèles : Hunter S. Thompson et Marlon Brando.

2003–2007 Prend un nouveau départ en incarnant Jack Sparrow dans la superproduction des studios Disney, *Pirates des Caraïbes*. Les années passées à jouer les excentriques et à défier les genres sont récompensées par l'immense succès populaire de ce personnage de pirate efféminé et déjanté.

PORTRAIT FOR 'PIRATES OF THE CARIBBEAN: AT WORLD'S END' (2007)

4
FILMOGRAPHY

FILMOGRAFIE

FILMOGRAPHIE

A Nightmare on Elm Street (dt. *Nightmare –* *Mörderische Träume,* **fr.** *Les Griffes de la nuit,* **1984)**
Glen Lantz. Director/Regie/réalisation: Wes Craven.

Private Resort (dt. *Der Superaufreißer,* **1985)**
Jack. Director/Regie/réalisation: George Bowers.

Slow Burn (TV movie/Fernsehfilm/fr. *Morts en* *eau trouble,* **téléfilm, 1986)**
Donnie Fleischer. Director/Regie/réalisation: Matthew Chapman.

Platoon (1986)
Private/soldat Gator Lerner. Director/Regie/ réalisation: Oliver Stone.

21 Jump Street (TV series/Fernsehserie/série TV, 1987–1990)
Officer/agent Tom Hanson. Director of Pilot/Regie des Pilotfilms/réalisation de l'épisode pilote: Kim Manners.

Cry-Baby (1990)
Wade "Cry-Baby" Walker. Director/Regie/ réalisation: John Waters.

Edward Scissorhands (dt. *Edward mit den* *Scherenhänden,* **fr.** *Edward aux mains d'argent,* **1990)**
Edward Scissorhands/Edward aux mains d'argent. Director/Regie/réalisation: Tim Burton.

Freddy's Dead: The Final Nightmare (dt. **Nightmare 6 –** *Freddy's Finale,* **fr.** *La Fin de* *Freddy, l'ultime cauchemar,* **1991)**
Guy on TV/Teenager im Fernsehen/un ado à la télé. Director/Regie/réalisation: Rachel Talalay.

Arizona Dream (1993)
Axel Blackmar. Director/Regie/réalisation: Emir Kusturica.

Benny & Joon (dt. *Benny und Joon,* **1993)**
Sam. Director/Regie/réalisation: Jeremiah Chechik.

What's Eating Gilbert Grape (dt. *Gilbert Grape –* *Irgendwo in Iowa,* **fr.** *Gilbert Grape,* **1993)**
Gilbert Grape. Director/Regie/réalisation: Lasse Hallström.

Ed Wood (1994)
Edward D. Wood jr. Director/Regie/réalisation: Tim Burton.

Don Juan DeMarco (1994)
Don Juan. Director/Regie/réalisation: Jeremy
Leven.

**Nick of Time (dt. *Gegen die Zeit*, fr. *Meurtre en
suspens*, 1995)**
Gene Watson. Director/Regie/réalisation: John
Badham.

Dead Man (1995)
William Blake. Director/Regie/réalisation: Jim
Jarmusch.

Donnie Brasco (1997)
Donnie Brasco/Joseph D. "Joe" Pistone. Director/
Regie/réalisation: Mike Newell.

The Brave (1997)
Raphael. Director/Regie/réalisation: Johnny Depp.

**Fear and Loathing in Las Vegas (fr. *Las Vegas
Parano*, 1998)**
Raoul Duke/Hunter S. Thompson. Director/Regie/
réalisation: Terry Gilliam.

**The Ninth Gate (dt. *Die neun Pforten*,
fr. *La Neuvième Porte*, 1999)**
Dean Corso. Director/Regie/réalisation: Roman
Polanski.

**The Astronaut's Wife (dt. *Die Frau des
Astronauten*, fr. *Intrusion*, 1999)**
Commander/commandant Spencer Armacost.
Director/Regie/réalisation: Rand Ravich.

Sleepy Hollow (1999)
Ichabod Crane. Director/Regie/réalisation: Tim
Burton.

**The Man Who Cried (dt. *In stürmischen Zeiten*,
fr. aka *Les Larmes d'un homme*, 2000)**
Cesar. Director/Regie/réalisation: Sally Potter.

**Before Night Falls (dt. *Bevor es Nacht wird*,
fr. *Avant la nuit*, 2000)**
"Bon Bon"/Teniente Victor/lieutenant Victor.
Director/Regie/réalisation: Julian Schnabel.

**Chocolat (dt. *Chocolat – Ein kleiner Biss genügt!*,
fr. *Le Chocolat*, 2000)**
Roux. Director/Regie/réalisation: Lasse Hallström.

Blow (2001)
George Jung. Director/Regie/réalisation: Ted
Demme.

From Hell (2001)
Inspector/inspecteur Frederick Abberline.
Director/Regie/réalisation: Albert Hughes, Allen
Hughes.

Lost in La Mancha (2002)
Johnny Depp. Directors/Regie/réalisation: Keith
Fulton, Louis Pepe.

**Pirates of the Caribbean: Curse of the Black
Pearl (dt. *Fluch der Karibik*, fr. *Pirates des
Caraïbes, la malédiction du Black Pearl*, 2003)**
Captain/capitaine Jack Sparrow. Director/Regie/
réalisation: Gore Verbinski.

**Once Upon a Time in Mexico (dt. *Irgendwann in
Mexiko*, fr. *Il était une fois au Mexique*, 2003)**
Sands. Director/Regie/réalisation: Robert Rodriguez.

**Secret Window (dt. *Das geheime Fenster*,
fr. *Fenêtre secrète*, 2004)**
Mort Rainey. Director/Regie/réalisation: David
Koepp.

**Finding Neverland (dt. *Wenn Träume fliegen
lernen*, fr. *Neverland*, 2004)**
J. M. Barrie. Director/Regie/réalisation: Marc
Forster.

Ils se marièrent et eurent beaucoup d'enfants (eng. *Happily Ever After*, dt. *Happy End mit Hindernissen*, 2004)
Stranger/Fremder/L'inconnu. Director/Regie/réalisation: Yvan Attal.

The Libertine (fr. *Rochester, le dernier des libertins*, 2004)
John Wilmot, 2nd Earl of Rochester/der zweite Graf von Rochester/2ᵉ comte de Rochester. Director/Regie/réalisation: Laurence Dunmore.

Charlie and the Chocolate Factory (dt. *Charlie und die Schokoladenfabrik*, fr. *Charlie et la chocolaterie*, 2005)
Willy Wonka. Director/Regie/réalisation: Tim Burton.

Corpse Bride (dt. *Tim Burton's Corpse Bride – Hochzeit mit einer Leiche*, fr. *Les Noces funèbres*, 2005)
Victor Van Dort (Voice/Stimme/voix). Director/Regie/réalisation: Tim Burton.

Pirates of the Caribbean: Dead Man's Chest (dt. *Pirates of the Caribbean – Fluch der Karibik 2,*

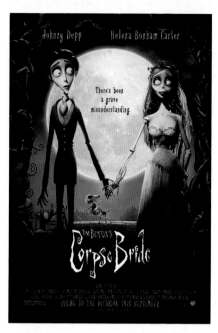

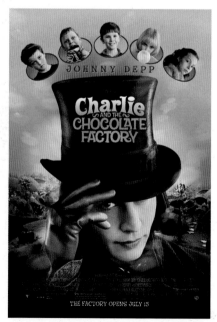

fr. *Pirates des Caraïbes, le secret du coffre maudit*, 2006)
Captain/capitaine Jack Sparrow. Director/Regie/réalisation: Gore Verbinski.

Pirates of the Caribbean: At World's End (dt. *Fluch der Karibik – Am Ende der Welt*, fr. *Pirates des Caraïbes, jusqu'au bout du monde*, 2007)
Captain/capitaine Jack Sparrow. Director/Regie/réalisation: Gore Verbinski.

Sweeney Todd: The Demon Barber of Fleet Street (dt. *Sweeney Todd – Der teuflische Barbier aus der Fleet Street*, fr. *Sweeney Todd, le diabolique barbier de Fleet Street*, 2007)
Sweeney Todd. Director/Regie/réalisation: Tim Burton.

Public Enemies (2009)
John Dillinger. Director/Regie/réalisation: Michael Mann.

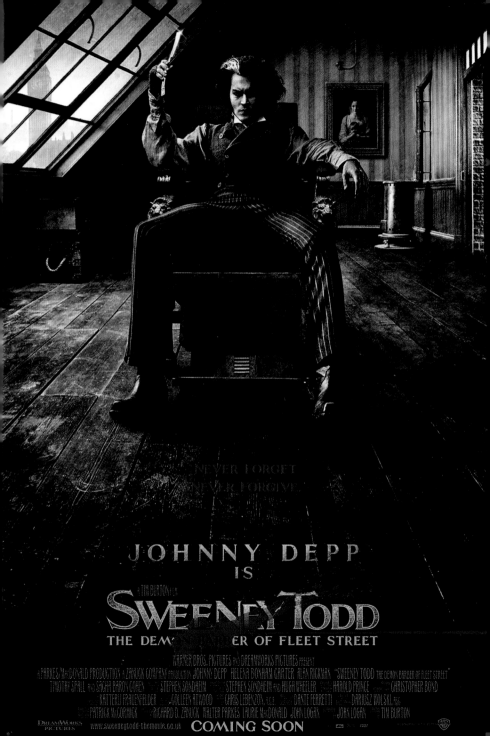

BIBLIOGRAPHY

Goodall, Nigel: *What's Eating Johnny Depp?* London, 2004.
Heard, Christopher: *Depp.* Toronto, 2001.
Heinzelmeier, Adolf: *Johnny Depp: Der sensible Don Juan.*
  München, 1996.
Hunter, Jack (Ed.): *Johnny Depp: Movie Top Ten.* London, 1999.
Johnston, Nick & Heffe, Claire: *Johnny Depp.* Paris, 2006.
Meikle, Denis: *Johnny Depp: A Kind of Illusion.* London, 2004.
Pomerance, Murray: *Johnny Depp Starts Here.* New Brunswick, NJ,
  2005.
Reisfeld, Randi: *Johnny Depp.* New York, 1989.
Robb, Brian J.: *Johnny Depp: A Modern Rebel.* London, 2004.
Romano, Jason: *Johnny Depp.* Lausanne, 2005.
Seitz, Alexandra: *Johnny Depp.* Berlin, 2007.

IMPRINT

© 2009 TASCHEN GmbH
Hohenzollernring 53, D-50 672 Köln
www.taschen.com

Editor/Picture Research/Layout: Paul Duncan/Wordsmith Solutions
Editorial Coordination: Martin Holz, Cologne
Production Coordination: Nadia Najm, Cologne
German translation: Thomas J. Kinne, Nauheim
French translation: Anne Le Bot, Paris
Multilingual production: www.arnaudbriand.com, Paris
Typeface Design: Sense/Net, Andy Disl and Birgit Eichwede,
Cologne

Printed in China
ISBN: 978-3-8365-0849-0

To stay informed about upcoming TASCHEN titles, please
request our magazine at www.taschen.com/magazine or write
to TASCHEN, Hohenzollernring 53, D-50672 Cologne, Germany;
contact@taschen.com; Fax: +49-221-254919. We will be happy to
send you a free copy of our magazine, which is filled with infor-
mation about all of our books.

All the photos in this book, except for those listed below, were
supplied by The Kobal Collection.
David Del Valle, The Del Valle Archives, Los Angeles: 56, 58, 61.
Columbia TriStar/defd-images: Cover.
Thanks to Dave Kent, Phil Moad and everybody at The Kobal
Collection for their professionalism and kindness.